MASTERS'
KUNG FU

MASTERS'
KUNG FU

**An official book of the
Martial Arts Commission**

Simon Lau

PELHAM BOOKS

First published in Great Britain by
Pelham Books Ltd
44 Bedford Square
London
WC1B 3DP
1986

*British Library Cataloguing in
Publication Data*
Lau, Simon
    Masters kung fu.
    1. Kung fu
    I. Title
    796.8′159   GV1114.7

ISBN 0-7207-1682-9

Edited by Wendy Slemen
Designed and produced by
The Bowerdean Press Ltd.
London SW11

Typeset by Southern Positives and
Negatives (SPAN), Lingfield, Surrey
Printed and bound in England by
R. J. Acford, Chichester, Sussex.

The Martial Arts are potentially
dangerous: the author, producers and
publishers will accept no liability for
damage or injuries resulting from the
performance of techniques described in
this book.

Contents

Foreword

It was never my intention to become a martial artist, but I suppose few people start life with a clear picture of the path they will eventually follow. In my case, both my family and the monastery in which I was taught hoped that I would become a Buddhist monk and seek Enlightenment. It is ironic that although I have given up the formal study of religion, the alternative path I chose – that of martial art – has taken me along the same route.

Please do not think me immodest if I compare myself with masters who have gone before but it is nevertheless a fact that while such legendary figures as Ta Mo took up the martial arts to help them study their religion, I have taken the opposite road and found that the assiduous practice of martial art has deepened my understanding of life.

Like many young men I started training in the martial arts with the idea of becoming good at fighting. I might have continued with this shallow approach if circumstances had not led me to depend on the martial arts as an anchor. As it was, I found myself in a strange country, hampered by my inability to speak its language, so I therefore had to turn inwards and the martial arts became my discipline.

I undertook rigorous training as a way of fighting off frustration and lack of company, working at it with an intensity I had never generated before. Nothing happened at once. Only after years of this soul-destroying effort

did I begin to see the meaning of what I was doing. I ceased to be concerned about the perfection of my technique and concentrated instead on understanding its fundamental principles. Although my techniques looked little different, they were much more powerful and not so physically damaging.

Those years of effort moulded my approach to the martial arts. Without them I would have become a mere technician, doing the movements without knowing them. I have therefore come to regard this method of training as effective, certainly so far as I am concerned. There may be other ways to train but I do not know them. I believe that ability is forged through application; the greater the application, the greater the ability gained.

Ninety minutes twice a week will certainly teach you something, but do not expect it to turn you into a martial arts master. You may eventually learn the techniques but the absence of mental commitment will cripple their true application. It is as important to train the mind as it is the body. The person who becomes physically very adept but does not train his mind may well turn out to be a bully. The timid student who is frightened of others may learn to use techniques very effectively but he will remain a coward.

Some people ask me, 'What is the best martial art to follow?' I always answer that the art itself is unimportant; it is only as good as the person practising it. This book is about wing chun kuen and my interpretation of it but the style is incidental to the real purpose of the book, which could be about any martial art.

My purpose in writing lies beyond teaching you technique. I hope to inculcate in you, the reader, the motivation to become a martial artist rather than someone who merely practises the martial arts.

Simon Lau
Futshan province

Christmas 1985

Introduction

> *'If I take care of my character, my reputation
> will take care of itself.'*

I began training in the martial arts when I was about 12. My first teacher was my older brother, Anthony Lau, who in turn learned it from a friend, Mui Yut. Mui Yut was the student of Yip Man, the last grandmaster of wing chun kuen and Bruce Lee's teacher. Anthony was learning it for the same reason that many Chinese do – self defence. Few young Chinese take it up for its sporting or medicinal values and I was no exception. I wanted to be able to take care of myself.

The techniques passed on to me were only a half-learned hodgepodge but they were interesting enough to whet my appetite, so I began to study at Kowloon wing chun kuen school taught by Yip Man. Of course, when I started training, I knew little about any school of martial art and it is pure coincidence I ended up in that style.

My family were not altogether happy at my taking up the brawling art of the streetfighter. They had hoped to see me become a Buddhist monk and enrolled me in the Kowloon monastery school where my given name was Ji Fook. For six years I studied hard at Buddhist philosophy and religious instruction, but once accepted into Yip Man's club I became a very enthusiastic pupil of the Chinese martial arts.

I found Yip Man a modest and warm-hearted man. His humility and obvious wisdom quickly won the respect and confidence of his students.

When I was 18 I won a scholarship to Alberta University in Canada to study for a diploma in industrial administration, but the language barrier proved impossible to overcome. After only a short time I left for England where I enrolled as a student nurse at Goodmayes Hospital. I was still so isolated by my poor grasp of English that all I could turn to was my wing chun kuen training.

The only place I could find for training at that time was an unheated cycle shed with holes in the wall and a damp, filthy, concrete floor. Equipped with a sandbag and speedball, this became my first English gymnasium. Four hours every day I trained myself to the limits of endurance, often skipping meals to get enough training time.

In winter, the shed got so cold that the damp sand in the punching bag froze solid. I pounded the solid block with 200 or more full power punches with either hand. With no boxing gloves or bandages to ease the impact, the first blows drove needles of pain into the knuckles, but soon the cold numbed all feeling and allowed the exercise to continue. A six-mile run every day built my stamina and provided central heating to raise my body temperature until it could tolerate the harsh training conditions. The hospital shift system meant that I had to train at all sorts of strange hours and forcing myself to go to the makeshift gymnasium was the hardest part of all.

Fortunately my English was steadily improving. I soon discovered the existence of martial art clubs in London, but came away disappointed with the standards. Their teachers could not match my speed or strength and, frankly, they seemed weak by comparison. Finding no teacher to train under in wing chun kuen, I eventually decided to set up my own club, teaching a small group of staff at Goodmayes Hospital. In 1973, I discovered a health club in Ilford where the owner, a wrestler, was interested in opening a martial arts section. Soon the club had 15 keen students training among the weight-lifting gear.

News of the club spread and there were soon queues of people applying to join. Acting on the advice of students, I hired cheaper premises and set up an independent club. Once established, I decided to join the British Kung Fu Council, the governing body for the Chinese martial arts in Britain and a founder member of the Martial Arts Commission, which is recognised by the Sports Council. At Seymour Hall in London, my senior students gave a display of wing chun kuen and I was fortunate to be immediately offered membership.

My first public demonstration took place in front of 400 students in the British Council Students' Union, Portland Place. This was followed by a guest appearance at a Bruce Lee Convention where my demonstration kindled the enthusiasm of the 3000-strong audience. Soon afterwards, applications for membership were arriving by the sackload, but without a proper place to train, many applicants could not be affiliated.

Despite this small measure of success, I continued to train myself as hard as ever and decided to look outwards beyond the confines of wing chun kuen. I had several practice sessions with Tyrone Whyte – one of Britain's leading international karate athletes – and exchanged valuable knowledge of techniques. I next made a comparative study of wing chun kuen, karate, and taekwondo, incorporating their best elements into my own practice. A word of caution: students must not be tempted to study more than one martial art at a time. Select one and train in it until you achieve a high standard. Only then will you have a strong platform from which to study other arts.

In 1980 I decided to devote myself to full-time training. With much trepidation I left the security of my job and bought a training hall. At first the facilities were very spartan – almost like the old cycle shed – with no heating and a rough floor. My training hall is now well established and I am fortunate to have a thriving membership.

I have always been very interested in television work and was selected by the producers of the BBC programme, *'The Way of the Warrior'*, to depict the epitome of hard Chinese martial art. The producers were very happy with what they filmed and I was photographed for their excellent book of the series. My next appearance was as the 'muscle power' in Goldcrest's series, *'The Living Body'*. To get the part, I had to compete with martial artists of other disciplines. When a high-speed camera was used to measure the speed of my punch, I was found to throw the fastest technique of the group auditioned.

As a result of this media exposure, students from all over the world have trained with me and I currently have clubs in Chicago and Gothenburg. My main problem now is trying to find enough time to fit everything in.

The following advice applies to students of all martial arts, not just those of wing chun kuen. Use it as the basis for your training.

1. Always be forthright and open in your practice. Do not boast of any skills you may have; there is always someone who is better. Conversely, do not be dispirited if you are not as good as the student next to you. Set your own standards and work within them, trying to improve on your own performance of the previous session.

2. Do not become preoccupied with gaining coloured belts. Grading examinations have both good and bad sides. On the positive side, they can give you a sense of modest achievement in having reached a goal. On the negative side, they can lead to an unhealthy preoccupation with advancement. Never forget that the grade held should reflect true ability. The senior grade, if properly obtained, should always indicate greater strength and technical development than the lower grade. A grade obtained without effort is without value.

3. Competition is not the be-all and end-all of practice, but merely a small part. Sport is positive in that it promotes the healthy striving of two individuals each attempting to measure his ability, within the rules, against the other. It is negative when its importance becomes exaggerated, resulting in an unfortunate narrowing or specialisation of practice.

4. Remember to have respect for the teacher and for the other students. Everyone is learning together, although some are a little further along the unending path than others.

5. Practise to find your real self. Martial art is not just a way of being able to fight; it is also a means of self-realisation and, practised in the right spirit, it will transform your personality in a positive way.

6. There is no end to training. Never think you have mastered a technique or you will cease to improve.

History of wing chun kuen

It is important to understand exactly what martial art is. Many students like to know how their particular martial art came to take its current form.

China has a long history of civilisation and a great tradition of martial art practice. It has suffered from innumerable wars during which much written tradition was lost. Existing historical sources generally relate to the more recent past. Little is known about early martial art practice, but myths and legends abound.

We can make some fairly safe generalisations about early Chinese martial art practice. There must have been a great deal of hand-to-hand combat and, where weapons were more or less similar, only the ability (or luck) of the combatants decided the winner. Fighting effectively with weapons like swords or clubs means knowing the principles of evasion, blocking, distance, timing, and tactics. Compare this with simply pointing a gun and pulling the trigger.

A successful warrior of those times would be well armed, he would not be in the wrong place at the wrong time, and he would be able to use his chosen weapon with a high degree of ability and cunning. This is the essence of martial or military art.

You can, of course, prevail against the most skilled soldier if you overwhelm him with sheer weight of numbers. This is the principle of 'cannon fodder'. In the accounting practice of war this can be a costly exercise, needing a very large pool of victims to sustain it.

Probably the early Chinese armies, like modern ones, consisted of both types of warriors. The more skilled variety – the shock troops – would be built up during periods of peace, when there was time to follow a longer training programme. With onset of war and attrition of troops, hastily trained conscripts would be pressed into service.

The tactics employed by the skilled warrior would be those tested and found effective on the battlefield. The techniques which did not work died with their inventors. Some good techniques were also lost when innovators found themselves facing impossible odds. Nevertheless, many were recorded and passed on by word of mouth or through written manuals to which reference can still be made today.

The continuing rigorous testing of military technique ensured its effectiveness within the conditions prevailing at the time. Nowadays conditions are different and there are no longer the same opportunities for testing new techniques. We must therefore be on our guard against so-called modern martial arts.

It seems obvious to me that the method of training in any martial art must be as lifelike as possible if it is to benefit the warrior. If, for safety's sake, you allow soldiers to practise techniques with a wooden sword, the practice weapon must be weighted like a real one. If that is not done, slight changes in technique will occur which enhance use of the dummy weapon yet are inappropriate for the real one.

Similarly, if safety rules are introduced, actual battle effectiveness can be lost. If, for example, the groin is designated as a prohibited target during practice, the soldier may overlook the need to protect it, with possibly fatal results on the battlefield. Martial art is not the same as combat sport. The latter is a game loosely based on a martial art.

Chinese martial art is conspicuous for the large numbers of curious weapons which have appeared from time to time. Combat training must have taught the warrior how to use and deal with the more familiar types but an unconventional weapon requires a new response. Its user would have trained against conventionally armed opponents and therefore had a sound tactical advantage, at least until the novelty of the new weapon wore off and effective techniques for dealing with it were devised.

Chinese military history is also noteworthy for the early introduction of new weapon technologies. China had operational war rockets many years before Congreve introduced them to the West. The army which quickly utilised the latest weapon developments, then as now, must have gained a great initial advantage. Consider the chances of highly skilled sword-wielding soldiers advancing on a conscript army equipped with repeating rifles.

In close-quarter combat, weapons can be dropped or broken, so it is a good idea to have a knowledge of unarmed combat in reserve. Another reason for practising it is that it provides the means to capture an opponent rather than kill him. The system must work against an armoured warrior so it

標材定規矩方圓
乙丑仲冬
雲泉楊永績

禍至則身手敏捷
福標先生雅屬膺并正腕

13

needs both hard strikes and holds/trips/throws.

All but the smallest battles must be more than free-for-alls, with everyone out for himself. The simplest co-ordination of an army of soldiers requires an infrastructure of command and discipline to ensure that everyone goes to a particular place at a particular time. To reduce the possibility of conflicting directions, one person must control things. Since he cannot be in more than one place at a time, his commands must be relayed to soldiers in the field through a chain of command and communications.

The astute commander does not send a company of archers to meet swordsmen in hand-to-hand combat. He uses the archers to attack from a distance, to weaken the advance of the sword-bearers so they may be more easily ridden down by his rapid deployment force, the cavalry. Such utilisation is battlefield strategy, an essential part of martial art.

Not only the armed forces trained in martial art. Surprisingly, it was also practised by monks in some Chinese monasteries. The most famous of these was Siu Lum, nestling at the base of the northern slopes of Sungshan mountain in Teng Feng district, Hunan province.

Siu Lum may have been built as early as the fifth century AD at the order of Emperor Hsiao. Hsiao was much impressed with the Chan Buddhist teachings introduced to China from India by travelling Indian monks. The most famous of these was Ta Mo, a legendary figure said to have been a reincarnation of Buddha. He is credited by some with bringing about a significant change in Chinese martial arts through his teaching of the *Eighteen Lohan* style of martial art from which all subsequent Siu Lum forms are said to originate. Less enthusiastic historians claim only that he introduced two exercises to help the monks endure physical hardships.

In AD 535 Siu Lum was razed to the ground in the wars between the Northern and Southern Kingdoms but it was rebuilt by the Emperor Su. He named it Chiu Su, meaning 'climbing the hill' but the name reverted to Siu Lum in the seventh century. It was during the Tang dynasty (AD 618– 960) that Siu Lum became known as a centre for martial arts practice. Ancient stories report that the monks showed exceptional fighting ability in the service of the emperor and were accorded special status. A force of only 14 monks fought with conspicuous success for Emperor Tai Tung. Although he tried hard to persuade them to become trainers for his army, they returned to Siu Lum when the battle was over.

Seven centuries later, Siu Lum once more supplied the reigning emperor with military assistance. This time the small number of monks did not return after the battle for, despite their heroic efforts, they were swamped by numerically superior forces of Japanese. In AD 1674, a further force of monks went to the aid of Emperor Kang. He rewarded them by burning the monastery and massacring all but five of the monks. These men, who managed to preserve some of the teachings of Siu Lum, are referred to in Chinese mythology as the Five Ancestors.

Siu Lum was eventually rebuilt yet again, only to be damaged once more during Chiang Kai Shek's 1920s campaign to re-establish a united China. Following the Cultural Revolution of the 1960s monks have been allowed to return and the monastery is now a tourist attraction.

tshan Temple

 Man

In their heyday, the warrior monks of Siu Lum were renowned as experts in the use of unorthodox weapons. The six-foot staff, an effective weapon, became a favourite with the wandering monk. Three hundred year old comprehensive manuals for its use still exist; the most famous is, perhaps *Wu pei chih*, which was written by Mao Yuan Ye.

Buddhist monks are great travellers. During their peregrinations they introduced many and varied interpretations of martial art to the general population. The monks of Siu Lum taught a fighting system which relied on strong muscular effort. Accordingly it was named *ngoy gar*, the external system, to distinguish it from the less forceful internal system of *loy gar*. Internal systems are based on the Taoist philosophy, which predates Chan Buddhism.

The monks, who were innovative by nature, introduced numerous individual variations. Some studied the way animals fought and translated the techniques into human terms. Chinese martial art folklore has many tales of storks fighting bears and snakes.

The communities which benefited from instruction by the wandering monks also made alterations to what they were taught. Not all the famous Chinese boxers were monks or military men. It has been claimed that the more agile people of northern China favoured leg techniques, so there was a bias towards the development of kicks. The southern Chinese favoured solid systems which allowed fighting from a closer distance. We know that some ancient families developed secret variations of technique. Because of the secrecy which surrounds them, no one knows how many forms of Chinese martial art exist.

The history of my own martial art, wing chun kuen, begins with a legendary Buddhist nun called Ng Mui. Inspired by seeing a crane fighting with a snake, she originated a new style which became known as wing chun from the name of the young woman who was her student. The name means 'perpetual springtime'. Yim Wing Chun first passed the teachings on to her husband and later taught other people.

The style gained its greatest number of followers in Futshan, a town in the south of mainland China. This area is famous for its temples, its fine pottery, and wing chun kuen. The famous warrior monk Chih Shin is said to have fled there after the massacre which virtually wiped out Siu Lum. Futshan wing chun kuen became highly respected and produced some masters of great ability. One of these was Chan Wah Sun whose youngest student was the last grandmaster of wing chun kuen, Yip Man.

Yip Man, a native of Namhoi county, Kwangtung province, was only 13 when Chan Wah Sun died and he was obliged to continue his training under Ng Chung So. Yip Man went to St Stephens College in Hong Kong where he met Leung Bik, the eldest son of grandmaster Leung Jan, Chan Wah Sun's teacher. Leung Bik's method of training was slightly different. It overlayed elements of sophistication on the firm grounding provided by Chan Wah Sun.

After the war, Yip Man returned to his homeland and became police commissioner for Namhoi where he had numerous opportunities to test the techniques he had learned. There are many stories of how he scorned

15

the use of his service pistol, relying instead on unarmed techniques to take miscreants into custody. At the time of the Communist take-over in 1949, Yip Man returned to southern Hong Kong, settled there, and opened a martial arts club.

Yip Man's best-known student was the film star Bruce Lee.

Since the legendary founder of wing chun kuen was a woman, it is not surprising that the techniques are not very hard; that is, they do not require great strength to be effective. Wing chun kuen contains no superfluous techniques and has one of the smallest training syllabuses in Chinese martial art so it is possible to teach all the techniques in five years.

The cornerstone of effective combat is a fast, unthinking reaction which does not require the slowing mediation of the brain. An attack is sensed at the earliest stage and the counter is unhesitating, immediate and correct. It follows that the fewer techniques there are to learn, the quicker someone can become effective.

Martial art is widely practised in Hong Kong today but its association with cinema violence gives it a poor image and many families try to dissuade their younger members from taking it up. This is a pity, because properly taught martial art improves the student's character and health. There is much more to martial art than fighting; it is a philosophy and a set of related skills such as herbal medicine and bonesetting. If the teacher does not instil the correct philosophy, students are misled into actions which discredit martial art.

In Hong Kong, martial art clubs tend not to advertise. If they do, then sooner or later a student of a rival school will pay a visit and challenge the master to a fight. Good clubs have to be searched out, with only word-of-mouth recommendations to go on. Not all clubs teach good quality martial art, and those that do are generally the hardest to find and join.

If you succeed in finding a good club, your problems are not over. Sometimes the teacher will interview the applicant's parents or ask for references to find out about his character. This is not as silly as it sounds because martial art techniques can be very dangerous if they are used irresponsibly.

The term *kung fu* means the attainment of skill through training, and its application is by no means restricted to Chinese martial art. You can, for instance, say that a chef who can skilfully fillet a fish is showing *kung fu*. However, the term has gained widespread use as the colloquial name for Chinese martial art.

Developing latent power

'Simplicity is the ultimate attainment of art and the beginning of nature.'

You do not have to be a Charles Atlas to develop really powerful blows. Chinese are not among the biggest people in the world, so they have made up for their lack of mass by developing special techniques. These do not stem from purely physical principles but are derived from a harnessing of the body's natural energy. This is not to say that physical strength plays no part in the Chinese martial arts. In external schools (*ngoy gar*, or *wai chia* in Mandarin dialect) it certainly does.

Internal and external martial arts

There is a form of rigorous *ngoy gar* training called *ti po sam pai dah* which involves systematically hardening the whole of the body so it can withstand great punishment. Special methods of breathing which concentrate power are taught and the hands and feet are turned into bionic weapons capable of tearing the flesh from the body or burying the punch to the elbow in hard-packed sand. This most extreme form of physical training requires a regimen of training which would frighten off all but the most masochistic of followers.

All external martial arts try to explain the action of the body in terms of levers, muscles, and forces. How many times have you seen the expression 'Force equals mass multiplied by the square of the acceleration' as the rationale behind theories to make your strike more powerful? These theories are based on the assumption that the body behaves like a machine. Broadly speaking this may be true, but the body is a very complex structure whose operation cannot be wholly explained in simple physical terms and equations.

Groups which adopt these physical principles use many different and interesting ways to develop power. Sometimes a length of inner tube is used, with one end attached to the wrist and the other to a wallbar. Punching against its elasticity produces great strength but no focus. The difference between these two concepts can be best demonstrated with a punching bag.

The physically strong person punches the bag very hard and it swings violently. When the martial artist punches the bag it does not swing at all; rather, it kinks at the point of impact and may even split with the force of the blow. The ability to channel force in this way is the essence of true martial art. It marks the difference between sheer physical power and the skilful channelling of energy.

Physical martial arts develop truly awesome force by using highly specialised stances and complex interplays of body parts. But what happens if you have to defend yourself from a sitting position? Other arts specialise in a form of breathing to develop power. This again is effective only so long as you are not caught unawares. There are some fascinating martial art films which show the hero tensing every muscle in his body as he delivers a technique. Visually this is very exciting, but in practical terms it is not necessary.

Physical martial arts are concerned with improving the acceleration of techniques so they gather kinetic energy. This is all well and good, but do not forget that the greater the distance over which the technique travels, the easier it is to counter. More effective are short-range strikes for which wing chun kuen is justly famous. These travel over a very short distance – sometimes as little as a couple of centimetres – yet they develop the power other styles achieve only with a full extension of the arm. The short-range punch is much more difficult to block because it starts closer to its target.

If maximum benefit is to be gained from high-acceleration strikes, impact must be arranged when the speeding technique is reaching maximum acceleration. This causes the blow to explode on the target with a devastating result. If, however, you get the distance wrong, then either the technique is not up to full acceleration when it lands, or acceleration drops sharply as the limb fully extends.

Remember that in a real combat the opponent is unlikely to stand still and you will have little chance to get distance absolutely right.

Some martial arts recommend rotating the fist on impact to improve the force. This too is difficult to achieve when the target is moving. Unless you are expert at it, a broken wrist can easily be the result.

If you rely on purely physical principles to develop power, what happens when you grow old and begin to lose your strength? The answer lies in study of the internal or *loy gar* (*nei chia* in Mandarin) systems of Chinese martial art. The famous warrior-monks of Siu Lum trained in both systems, choosing first to study external martial art. This is well suited to the physical young person and its benefits become obvious at an earlier stage. On the other hand, internal systems suit the older person, someone perhaps a little less aggressive. The benefits, though great, take longer to appear. Wing chun kuen achieves a balance of both internal and external principles.

Natural power

Regardless of the system followed, the aim will be to harness the energy of the body and focus it with the will. The Chinese word for will, *ye*, means more than the intention to perform a technique. It is actually a state of being where a technique is used without conscious thought – as though the technique itself knows when to be released. To develop *ye* requires meditation and special exercises, all of which are covered later in this book.

Think of your body as a source of energy which you can direct using *ye*. The untrained person is not effective in channelling his energy into a punch, so its force is dispersed and the blow possesses little force.

Like the untrained person, light is random energy, flowing in all directions. If it is co-ordinated and channelled by mirrors and lenses, it becomes a beam of coherent light which can burn a hole through steel. It is this focusing of natural energy which is the key to strong techniques. Chinese call this natural force *chi*. A correct flow of vital energy is

necessary not only to develop the effectiveness of a blow, but also to enjoy a healthy life.

I think western people are sceptical about the existence of *chi* because it has a non-technical name. If I were to call it bio-energy it would be more readily accepted. Be that as it may, *chi* exists and can be produced by the living tissues of the body. Its production is linked to the physical wellbeing of the body. The healthier you are, the more vigorous is your flow of life energy. However, this energy is unspecialised; it needs to be directed if benefits are to be drawn from it.

The principle of *chi* is not entirely Chinese but is found also in Indian yoga. Kundalini yoga attempts to harness the body's natural energy through meditation, but its practice requires great care. If you approach it wrongly, it can have serious effects on your health. *Chi* is not entirely metaphysical but seems to be associated with known biological processes, especially of the oxidative kind. This is why people are seen training for *chi* development under trees in the early mornings. The air at this time is fresh and clean, recharging the body and soothing the mind.

By means of simple exercises and meditation, *chi* can be channelled through the body, so that a seemingly innocuous action becomes imbued with surprising power. The essence of wing chun kuen is manipulation of the *chi* and all training is directed to this point. I will go on to discuss various physical procedures to make your techniques more powerful, but these are the icing on the cake. Do not become preoccupied with the physics involved; if you do, your conscious thoughts will intrude and training will suffer. Just practise the techniques hard and your mind will become quiet. As it does so, it will increase in *ye*.

To concentrate force, start by breathing correctly. Many people use only their upper chests when they breathe whereas you should try to use your diaphragm and lower chest. Breathe normally and do not hyperventilate. This will assist the *chi* to flow through your organs. Next apply your mind to what you are doing. Visualise the technique and where you want it to go. Do not think of what you are going to eat for dinner, or whether you left the gas on. Concentrate totally on training and your techniques will gain in power.

By focusing your attention, you screen out superfluous thought and your mind becomes quiet. This is the ideal state for effective training because in the absence of any kind of mental conflict the mind can see the correct path to follow. The singlemindedness this generates allows the body to act directly and without hesitation.

Begin your physical training by squeezing your fist as tightly as possible. Help it to form the correct shape and tension by striking a punching bag, gently at first. Make the muscles go into spasm quickly on impact with the bag, clenching them tightly, then relaxing them again an instant later. The tighter you can squeeze the fist and the faster the contraction/ relaxation you achieve, the faster your follow-up technique can be launched.

In the wing chun kuen punch, the effectiveness of the fist depends to a large degree on how tight it is closed. This in turn relies on sudden contraction of the muscles of the forearm, with supinator longus and the flexor longus playing the largest part. The muscles of the upper arm, the biceps and triceps, do not take part; if they did, the action of the elbow would be slowed. Not only that, but using those muscles means putting too much body commitment into one technique. If it missed, how would you extricate yourself?

Do not allow the fist to rotate or the wrist to bend. Having tightened up the lower arm on impact, stiffen your elbow momentarily, to channel force into the opponent. If you leave your elbow loose at that point, some of the energy developed by your punch will pass back along the arm in what is called recoil. This must be avoided, so train the power of your elbow joint through sticking hands – a technique I will describe later in the book.

When force is generated in the lower arm only, the need for a specialised stance vanishes and you can no longer be caught out on the wrong foot. If your technique is correct, you can punch hard even when standing on one leg. This is very important because both combatants are constantly moving during a fight and you must be able to exploit a sudden opening.

Your whole body must be sufficiently resilient to counter an attack, so develop your shoulder muscles so they become strong enough to allow you to retain an effective guard under physical pressure. Train also with the elbow, using sticking hands as the exercise of choice.

Wing chun kuen is a complete system. If you practise all of its syllabus, the ability to strike with great force will develop in step. There is no need to practise supplementary routines. Sticking hands will develop your elbows and shoulders, while work with the pole will teach you how to externalise the force you are developing. The wooden dummy makes you capable of striking forcefully from any angle. Twirling butterfly knives helps to strengthen your wrists.

When you have developed and channelled your power, be careful how you use it. A properly trained wing chun kuen boxer develops great force so he is careful to adjust the impact to the area under attack. There is no need to destroy someone's face with a full-power punch; the technique can be pulled and still produce the desired result. On the other hand, the torso is a more resilient target which can receive a great deal of force without permanent injury.

Natural weapons of the body

Though the deadly art of *dim mok* is not seen much nowadays, there are places where it is taught. To practise it, students condition their hands and fingers so that they are capable of inflicting fearful damage. Attacks are made with the skill of a surgeon, applying just the right degree of force in the right part of the body to disrupt the flow of *chi*. Hours or days later, the apparently unharmed person succumbs to a sudden stroke, heart attack, or similar malfunction.

I suppose modern medicine would explain *dim mok* by saying that the attack produces a blood clot which then breaks free and travels in the blood stream until it blocks some critical blood vessel, perhaps one supplying the heart or brain. It is known that if you damage a muscle, a contraction or spasm occurs in the injured fibres. If the damage is severe, unharmed fibres contract in sympathy. This sympathetic contraction can cover a large area of the body. If the diaphragm is affected, breathing difficulties can follow.

A blow to the side of the neck can cause damage to the vagus, a very large nerve with many functions, one of which is to slow down the heartbeat. You do not have to be a genius to work out the effect of injury to the vagus.

Fortunately, knowledge of such dangerous techniques is severely restricted. Even without such deadly knowledge, the Chinese martial arts are effective enough.

The legendary nun Ng Mui, who founded wing chun kuen probably did not carry an arsenal of weapons with her. The art's weapons are the hands and feet, trained and used so that they are truly effective.

Hand weapons
The fist is the most commonly encountered body weapon, though it has a number of serious drawbacks. The skin covering the delicate bones of the knuckles is thin. A hard clout on unconditioned knuckles produces painful bruising that can take days to clear up. The skin is easily cut by teeth or torn by simple abrasion with a rough surface. Also, if the fingers aren't rolled tightly into the palm, the middle joints reach the target first and suffer painfully in consequence.

Do not squeeze your thumb inside your fingers. This is very dangerous because as the fist closes up on hard impact, the thumb can be forced inwards and dislocate. If you leave your thumb sticking out it will get caught in a sleeve. The untrained wrist can be weak and twist on impact, producing a sprain or fracture.

To avoid all these painful mistakes, first learn to make the fist properly, then condition it so it can be used hard without getting injured. Open your hand right out, extending thumb and fingers fully, then roll the fingers into the centre of the palm and close the fist, locking the index and second fingers down with the thumb.

Hold out your forearm with thumb uppermost and see that the fist is in line with the bones of the forearm. If you let the wrist turn in or out it will fold on hard impact. Ideally there should be a solid line of bone from elbow right through to knuckles, with no angles or deviations from a straight path.

Rest your forearm on a horizontal surface to show how the fist is carried. The knuckles of the fist do not lie in a straight line and it is clearly impossible to land with all four of them. In wing chun kuen we elect to strike with the lower three knuckles, leaving the index knuckle unused.

Once the fist is correctly formed and carried, it is held relaxed. If it is kept tight all the time, it will tie up too many muscles of the forearm and make the punching action too slow. As the fist connects, the muscles of the forearm contract tightly and the lower knuckles are driven forwards by a slight rocking of the wrist. This gives better penetration, more power, and less recoil (fig 1). The Cantonese name for front punch is *yat je jong kuen*.

The fist is thrown into the target by the action of the elbow, using the closing action of the fist and tightening of the forearm muscles to generate speed and power. Start with your elbow slightly bent and the hand relaxed and open (fig 2). Quickly straighten the elbow and begin closing the fingers into the palm (fig 3).

Do not close the fist too early or the punch will be robbed of its speed. As the punch makes first contact, tighten the muscles of the forearm quickly and as forcefully as you can (fig 4). Relax immediately after you strike.

All short-range straight thrusting techniques can be easily coupled together to produce a rain of fast, jolting strikes. The key to success is the

FIG 5

FIG 7

spring-like action of the striking limb. Do not snap the technique out with a powered delivery and a whiplash pull-back. This is very injurious to joints, muscles and tendons. When the arm is pulled back it must be by a non-passive spring action.

Stand in a straddle stance with your knees bent and both arms held well forwards at about shoulder height. The right hand is extended forwards, the left is pulled back slightly. Both hands are open *(fig 5)*. Start with a short right punch, clamping up the forearm muscles as it is delivered then instantly relaxing *(fig 6)*. Draw back the fist slightly and punch with the left hand as quickly as you can *(fig 7, 8)*. With a little practice you can punch really hard several times a second, but make sure you contract your arm muscles as you strike, otherwise the punches will be flabby and without real force.

FIG 9

If you practise regularly and hard, the speed at which you throw a punch will increase. If you can keep the upper arm relaxed, you will find that the punch tugs hard on the elbow. In extreme cases of high-speed punching the elbow joint can actually separate by as much as half an inch, yet without causing injury. In short-range punches only the arm is used, but when you are punching from further out, let the shoulder lead behind it *(fig 9)*.

FIG 10   FIG 11   FIG 12

One-knuckle fist, *fong nan kuen* in Cantonese, concentrates all the force of the blow into a single point, so it is a very effective technique indeed. To form the fist, close your hands in the normal way but leave the middle knuckle of your index finger projecting well forward. Close your fist, ensuring there are no air spaces. When you lock your thumb in, it should be impossible to drive the knuckle back. Punch as though doing front punch *(fig 10, 11, 12)*.

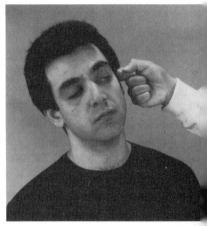

FIG

One-knuckle fist needs a lot of conditioning to allow forceful use without injury to the hand. It is not an easy technique for the novice and much practice is needed to form it quickly.

Targets for this technique are side of the head *(fig 13)*, windpipe, shoulder joints, and the viscera. Blows to windpipe, vagus, and voice box can prove lethal.

Multiple strikes with one-knuckle fist are performed exactly like those with front fist.

The circular punch *(geung jee kuen)* starts from the side of the body *(fig 14)* and swings around in a short, crisp arc *(fig 15)*, landing with the middle joints of the fingers *(fig 16)*. Lock the half-open fingers down with the thumb. It is not a long-distance technique and you must be careful not to lead with your face. As with one-knuckle punch, the impact area must be carefully conditioned to avoid damage, and your wrist must stiffen on impact.

Circular punch is very good for attacking ribs *(fig 17)*, side of head *(fig 18)*, or jaw.

FIG 15

FIG 16

FIG 17

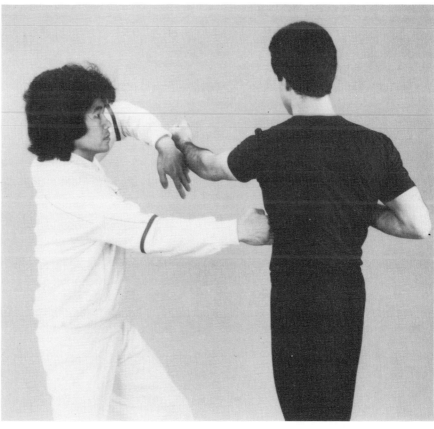

FIG 18

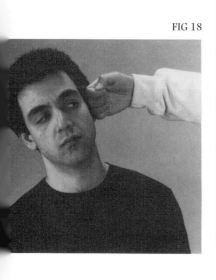

FIG 19

FIG 20

Back fist uses the same area of the knuckles as front fist. Make a normal, tightly rolled fist and deliver it with a hinge action of the elbow, striking either horizontally or vertically. (Actually, horizontal back fist is not found in traditional wing chun kuen.) When you are striking downwards, it is permissible to drop the elbow to add weight to the technique.

To practise vertical back fist (gwa choy), start from a right-stance, with your right elbow held high and your left palm-forwards behind it (fig 19). Raise your right wrist with a circular action, maintaining the left-hand guard (fig 20), and bring the strike in an arc until it is brought to a stop on the target (fig 21, 22).

FIG 21

FIG 22

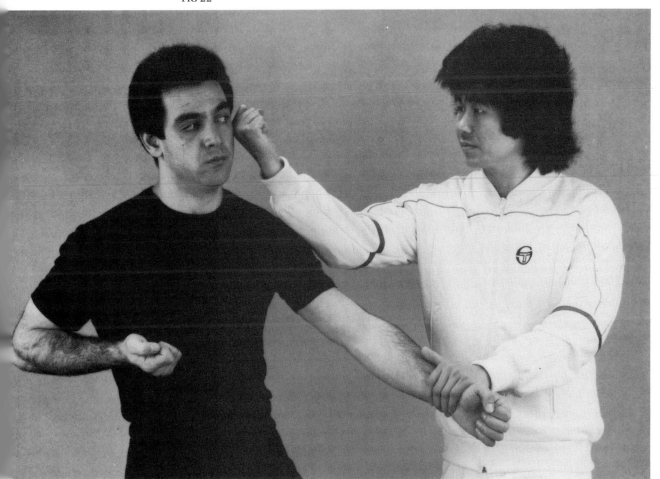

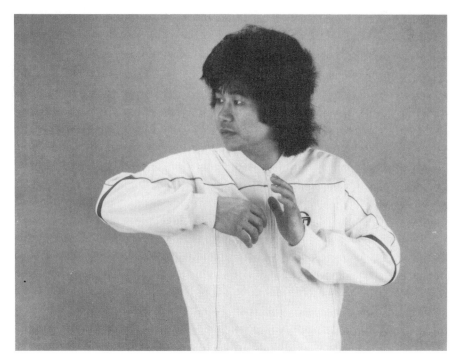

FIG 23

FIG 24

Start horizontal back fist *(wang kuen)* from a side-on position, raising and pointing your elbow at the target *(fig 23)*. Use your other hand as a guard and hold it palm-forward, thumb against chest, just behind the striking fist. Lean slightly into the strike and quickly unroll your elbow *(fig 24, 25, 26)*. Natural spring action of the elbow draws the strike quickly back after use.

FIG 25

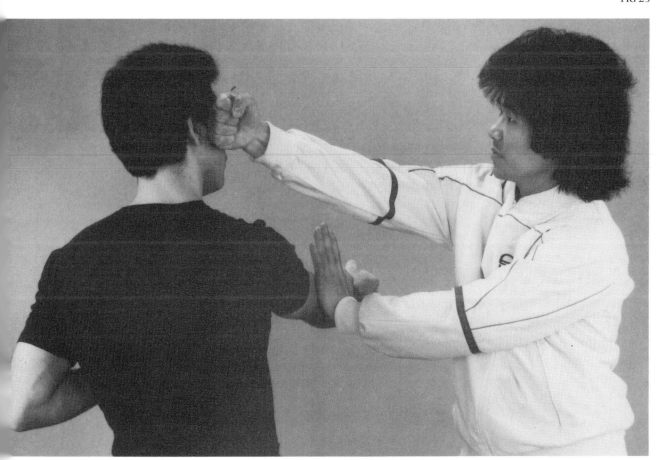

FIG 26

There is a variant of back fist which can be used to attack someone standing at your side. As with horizontal back fist, start by pointing your elbow at the target *(fig 27)* and unroll it to full extension, striking to the head *(fig 28)*. If you want to practise a multiple sideways back fist strike, bring the arm back quickly and drive it out again, but this time to midsection *(fig 29)*. Without pausing, draw it back and strike again, this time to the lower body *(fig 30)*. Practise this on both sides.

FIG 27

FIG 28

FIG 29

FIG 30

FIG 31

FIG 32

FIG 33   FIG 34

Forward-facing multiple back fist strikes use horizontal or inclined rotation of the forearms, similar to that used by a boxer working on a speedball. Carry both arms horizontally in front of your chest with hands open and palms facing back to the chest *(fig 31)*. Strike first with one back fist *(fig 32)* then draw it quickly back in a shallow arc, at the same time going over the top of it with the other *(fig 33, 34)*. This is a very effective short-range technique inside the opponent's guard.

Use back fist to attack the face and head, but be careful not to land on just one knuckle as this can cause injury.

Knife hand *(sau do)* can be used in a variety of ways. Impact is made with the narrow area between the base of the little finger and the wrist. Fingers must be stiffened on impact and the thumb turned in against the base of the index finger. Failure to do this will result in a weak strike with the fingers painfully rattling together.

The strike is delivered with a horizontal chopping motion during which the hand twists from palm facing upwards *(fig 35)* to palm downwards just before impact *(fig 36, 37)*. The edge of the hand is also used in a straight thrusting strike where, instead of a circular swinging action, the strike is made in a straight line like a punch *(fig 38, 39)*. The forearm rotates as it nears the target and the wrist is slightly flexed to present the striking area *(fig 40)*.

Thrusting knife hand *(chan sau)* can also be used in a multiple sequence. Hold both your arms unequally forward just above shoulder height and incline the palms upwards and inwards *(fig 41)*. Curl your fingers forward. Thrust the leading hand quickly forwards and, as the elbow is about to straighten, pull your hand into knife configuration, stiffening the wrist at the moment of impact *(fig 42)*. As soon as the hand touches the target it is withdrawn, and the second knife hand is sent on its way to the target *(fig 43, 44)*.

FI

FIG 35

FIG 36

F‌

FIG 38

FIG 39

36

FIG 42   FIG 43   FIG 44

Because of the narrowness of the impact area, the strike is very effective, especially when used against the throat, *(fig 45)* or neck *(fig 46)*. If it is used against the ribs, its profile allows it to penetrate between them, causing severe damage to the lungs and viscera.

FIG 45   FIG 46

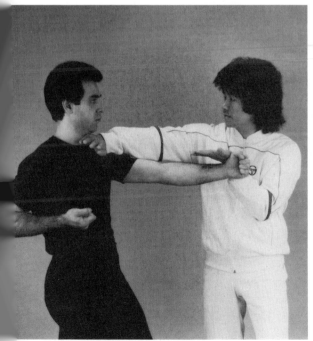
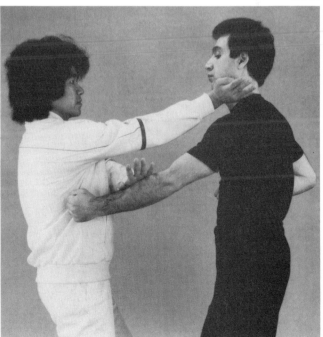

Ridge hand *(bui do)* uses the area between thumb and wrist as a weapon. Swing the arm into the target *(fig 47)*, keeping your elbow bent throughout. Use ridge hand as you move past the opponent, striking to groin, nose, throat *(fig 48)*, or neck.

Palm heel *(jing jeung)* is a very powerul thrusting technique which uses

FIG 47

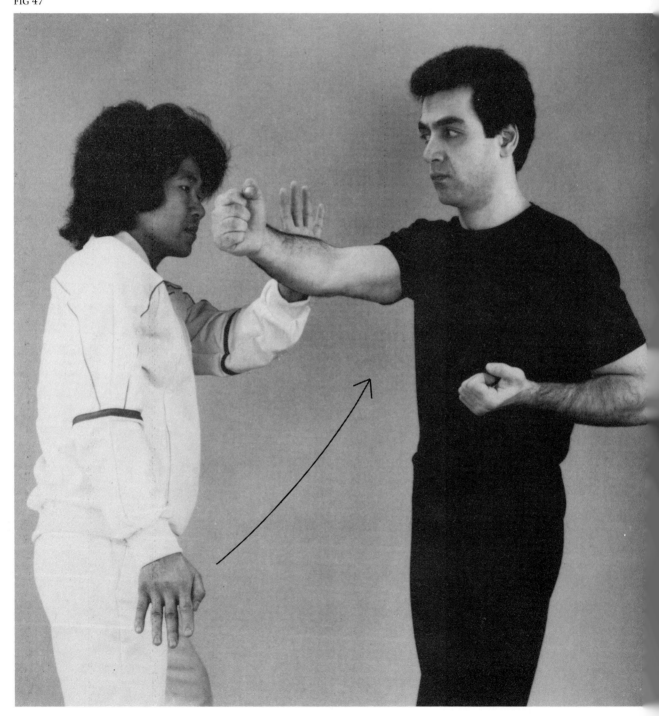

the pad of flesh at the base of the hand. There is little chance of wrist flexion. The palm plays an important role in certain kung fu schools and undergoes an especially rigorous form of conditioning which produces the iron palm. This makes the palm very hard indeed but can damage the hand's normal function.

FIG 48

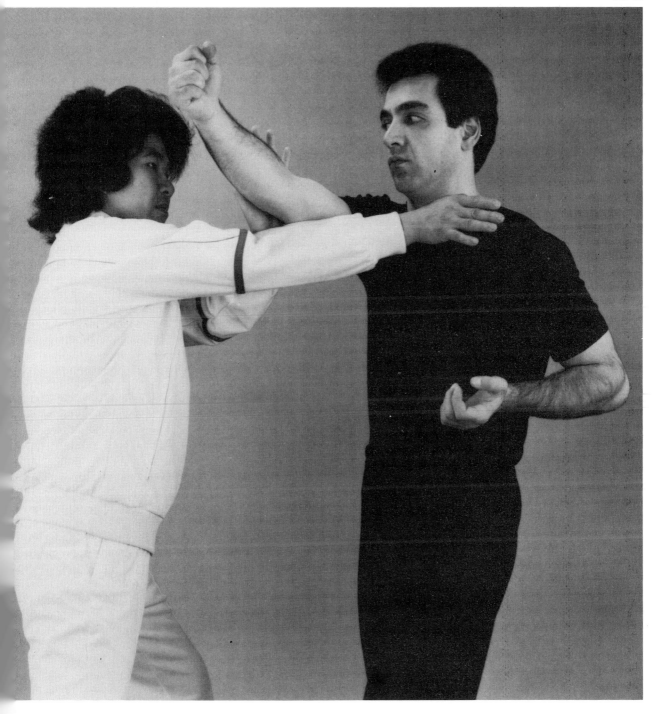

The action of the strike is the same as that for a punch. The arm is thrown at the target with fingers pulled part-way back *(fig 49)*. As they contact the opponent, the heel of the palm thrusts forward, propelled by the wrist and the locking of the forearm *(fig 50)*.

Like all thrusting arm techniques, palm heel can be coupled into multiple sequence of devastating power. Practise by holding your arms unequally

FIG 51   FIG 52   FIG 53

forward, hands open and palms facing away from you. Curl your fingers slightly and incline the palm of the leading hand forward *(fig 51)*. Drive it out from this position and as the fingers make first contact with the target, slam the heel of the hand forwards *(fig 52)*. Use a short, natural spring action to draw the strike back a couple of inches *(fig 53)*; as you do so, throw the second strike *(fig 54)*.

If delivery speed is low, the technique turns into a shove. The novice also often fails to tuck in his thumb, making the technique weak.

For a shorter-range palm heel strike *(yan jeung)*, a short swinging action can be used, keeping the elbow close to the body *(fig 55)*. Palm heel is very effective against the jaw *(fig 56)* and ribs *(fig 57)*.

FIG 55

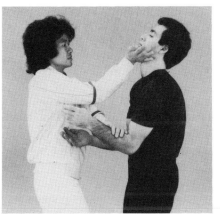

FIG 56

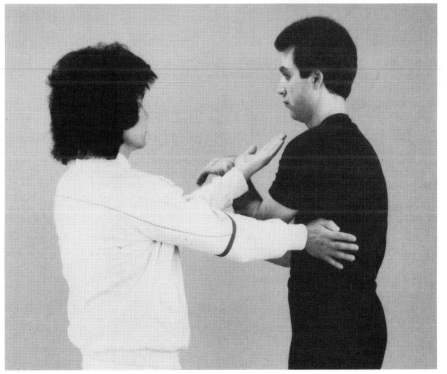

FIG 54

FIG 57

Spear hand *(biu ji)* is a speciality of wing chun kuen and there is a whole form devoted to its use. Unlike most wing chun kuen techniques, however, *biu ji* has a long-range application. Start with both arms quite close to your chest. The hands are open and both palms are turned to the floor *(fig 58)*. Use your elbow to bring the forearm up in a short arc and throw it into the target *(fig 59)*. Your wrist is quite relaxed until close to the target, when it is suddenly driven out *(fig 60)*. Power is generated by a combination of elbow and hip action.

Do not leave your fingers relaxed, or the technique will lose power. Remember also to fold in your thumb. *Biu ji* is used to attack the eyes *(fig 61)* or throat.

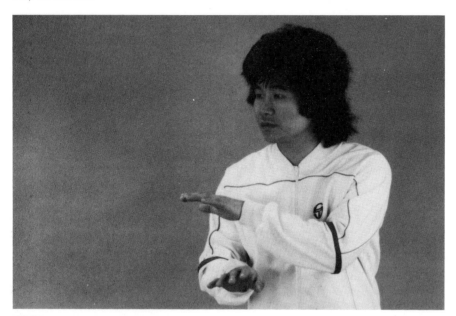

FIG 58

FIG 59

FIG 60

FIG 61

FIG 62   FIG 63   FIG 64

Elbow strikes are very effective at close range. The elbow is already hard and needs little conditioning. There are two types of elbow strikes, the first travelling horizontally, the second vertically.

To practise horizontal strike *(pai jan)*, start with the left foot slightly forwards and bring your left hand palm upwards across your midsection. Your striking arm is also held palm upwards at the right side *(fig 62)*. Raise your right elbow vertically until it is at the desired height *(fig 63)*, then swing it around and across the body in a short, horizontal arc *(fig 64)*.

Vertical elbow strike *(kup jan)* uses a slightly different action though it starts from the same position *(fig 65)*. This time raise your elbow up and close to the side of your head, but do not let it swing wide at any time *(fig 66, 67)*. Once it is at maximum height, swing it forward and down with a short, powerful movement that wipes it down the front of the opponent's face and on to his breast bone *(fig 68)*.

FIG 66

FIG 68

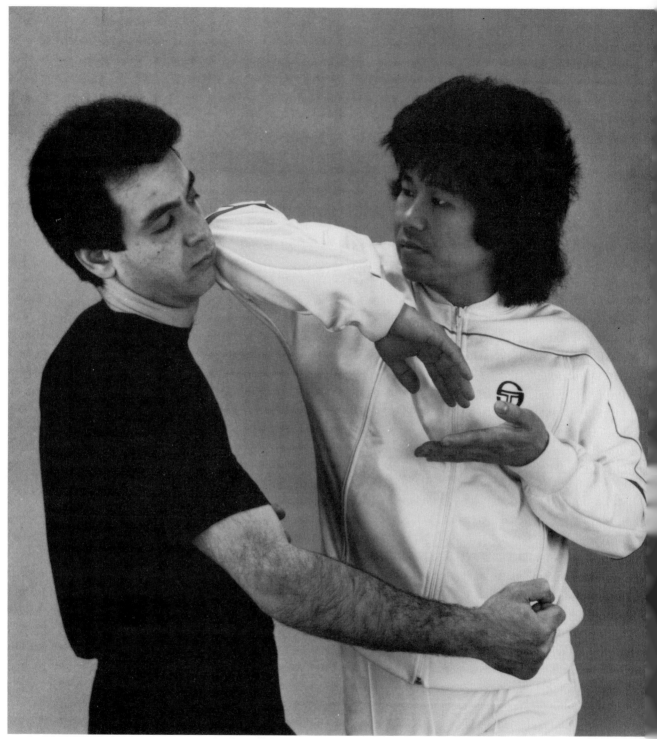

FIG 69

Do not be tempted to tighten your biceps as you deliver the strike. This will slow the movement down and make you too committed to it. Use elbow strike against the face *(fig 69)* or body *(fig 70)*.

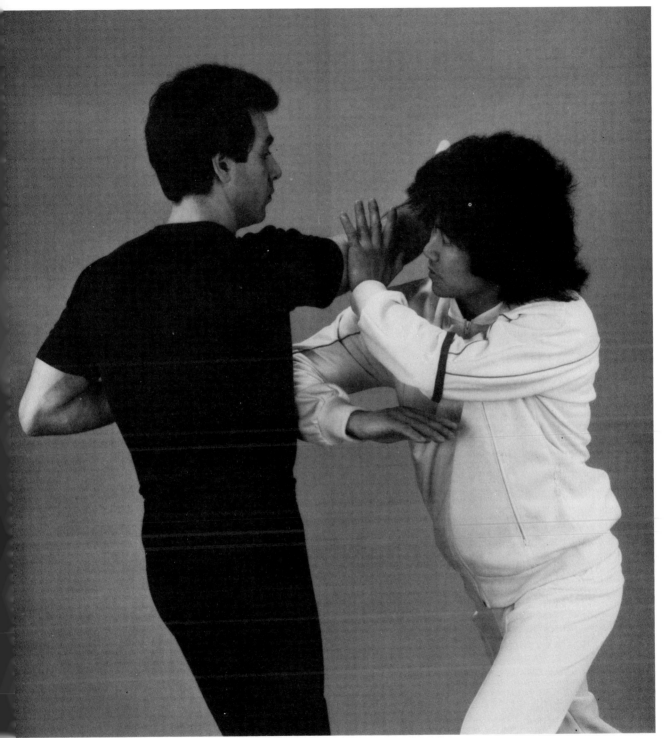

FIG 70

47

FIG 71   FIG 72

Leg weapons

Since wing chun kuen's effectiveness is biased towards close-range combat, leg techniques are highly specialised. Given that you are standing very close to your opponent in a pushing, jostling mêlée, the last thing you need to do is stand on one leg longer than is necessary. Although the kick is more powerful than the punch, it is slower.

There are occasions when a powerful kick is a useful complement to your response, but never use it above chest height. Typical targets for the wing chun kuen kick are thighs, groin, lower stomach (*fig 71*), chest, knees (*fig 72*), shin, and instep.

The first kick technique is front thrust kick (*jik dang ger*). To practise this, stand in a forward-facing fighting stance. Simultaneously transfer your weight forwards and raise your back knee, bringing it forward and up. The knee must raise as high as the kick's target (*fig 73*). As the knee reaches the correct height, thrust the foot out in an arc, aiming it heel first at the target. The foot turns naturally outwards and impact is made with the heel (*fig 74*). After impact, draw the foot back quickly to retain balance.

When you do this kick, keep your body back and your shoulders low and bring your knee up to the correct height (*fig 75*). The kick is smooth in operation; try to avoid jerky movements because they slow down the kick and ruin your balance. Remember, all the power is generated locally, in the ankle and foot, so do not let other parts of the body interfere. Kick to the centre of the opponent's body (*fig 76*). Novices often kick wide and not only miss the target but leave their groin open to counter-attack. Do not lean as you deliver the kick or your balance can be upset.

FIG 73   FIG 74

FIG 75   FIG 76

49

Twisting thrust kick *(yoot ying ger)* employs a slightly different action and is used when the opponent is not directly in front of you. It takes time to set up special stances to meet new situations but the versatility of wing chun kuen means that you can attack anyone standing anywhere in range without having to shuffle your feet about.

Face the target at an angle and transfer your weight forwards *(fig 77)*. As before, bring your back foot up to and across your front *(fig 78)*, then thrust it straight out at the target. Your hips are forward-facing as the kick strikes home with the heel and your foot is inclined outwards *(fig 79)*.

There is a variant of twisting thrust kick *(tong ger)* in which the hips turn away and the foot rotates inwards. Again, face the target at an angle and bring your back leg forward – but this time bring it inwards too *(fig 80)*. Raise your knee across your body to kicking height *(fig 81, 81a)*, then drive it out heel-first into the target *(fig 82, 82a)*. Do not hunch your shoulders, but maintain an effective guard throughout.

Side thrust kick *(wang dun ger)* is used when the attacker is even further to your side. Bring your foot up until it just passes the leading knee *(fig 83, 84)*, then, instead of thrusting it out forwards, drive it directly out to the side, stamping out and down *(fig 85, 85a)*. Notice that for this technique I have permitted a slight degree of lean. Hold your defensive guard firmly throughout *(fig 86)*.

FIG 80   FIG 81   FIG 81A   FIG 82   FIG 82A

FIG 83   FIG 84   FIG 85   FIG 85A

FIG 86

Never leave any kick outstretched after impact; use the natural spring of the joint to bring it smartly back. Impact is made with the heel, so don't strike with the sole of the foot. Remember to make your ankle rigid on impact, otherwise it can cause a sprain.

FIG 87   FIG 88   FIG 89

FIG 90   FIG 91

Knee strike *(gwai sut)* is a very short-range technique which, though powerful, takes one leg off the floor in a potentially awkward situation. Use it carefully. There are two types of knee strikes, one where the knee travels vertically upwards in an arc and the other where it curves inwards.

The first is the more common. To practise it, stand facing your opponent *(fig 87)*, grab him by the shoulders or around the back of the neck *(fig 88)* and pull his upper body forwards and on to the strike *(fig 89)*. Keep your face out of the way and control your opponent's position with your arms.

The second type of knee strike is very effective against the side of the thigh. Use it when you are not directly in front of your opponent but do not pull him on to it. Leave your knee clear of your supporting leg as you swing it upwards and strike inwards at the target. If your opponent pulls you, so much the better; use his energy to increase the power of your attack *(fig 90)*.

A shin strike *(pak ger)* is particularly painful. You can use either the inside or the outside of the foot. To use the inside, kick with the back foot, keeping your foot low as it swings into your opponent's lower shin and ankle. Keep your weight back and do not lean forward *(fig 91)*. The outside of the foot is used in the same way as a side thrust kick except that you are stamping down on to the shin or instep *(choy ger)*. As before, keep your weight back and maintain an effective guard *(fig 92, 93)*.

FIG 92   FIG 93

Conditioning techniques

It is all very well having a fine looking technique, but will it work? For your techniques to be effective, you must not suffer damage through their use. Therefore you condition them so they become like bionic hammers, with only a light effort producing a great amount of force. This demands rigorous training over long periods and a full commitment. You will never become effective in wing chun kuen if you do not condition your hands and feet. There is no short cut.

A number of conditioning aids are used, the first of which is the impact pad. This is a flat canvas bag attached to the wall by hook and eye fasteners. It is filled with beans, sand, mixtures of the two, or ballbearings. Pads containing beans are less punishing than those with sand. Impact pads are used to condition the hands to the short jolting strikes which characterise wing chun kuen. Start with the softest pad and gradually work your way up.

Begin gently at first, with light impact, and aim to do at least 50 strikes on each hand. As your hands become conditioned, gradually increase the force of your blows. The jarring this causes makes your wrists strong and able to withstand impact.

Use a speedball to promote co-ordination and speed in hitting a moving target. The heavy punch bag has similar mass to that of a human being and striking it conditions your whole body. The punch bag is a popular training aid but you should avoid unbalanced conditioning; work out equally on all the equipment. Larger wall pads are used to condition the feet.

The wooden dummy is both a conditioning and a training aid. It is a stout pillar of wood with a number of mortise holes cut into it. These mortises receive tenons from three tapered spars which project out at various angles. Starting from the top, two spars project at a narrow angle to the centre line. Below them, a single spar projects on the centre line. A bent spar emerges from the centre line at a lower point. The three upper spars represent arms and the single lower spar, the leg and knee.

The central pillar – the body of the wooden dummy – is suspended on two springy wooden rails that are themselves firmly anchored. The latter provide a resilience to the dummy's responses (fig 94). Traditionally the dummy is unpadded, but I recommend using some padding around the body to allow longer and harder training.

The wooden dummy is not peculiar to wing chun kuen. It is recorded that monks at Siu Lum trained with a form of dummy. To cope with the large numbers of students, two long rows of dummies were sunk into the ground facing each other.

Hitting the dummy can prove quite punishing so begin gently. Always look at the top of the dummy as though it were the head of a real person. Try not to smack the dummy around, creating a lot of noise. If your techniques are correct, they will move the dummy forcefully but without a tremendous racket. Keep your arms close to the dummy at all times, just as you would in real combat to inhibit the opponent's freedom of

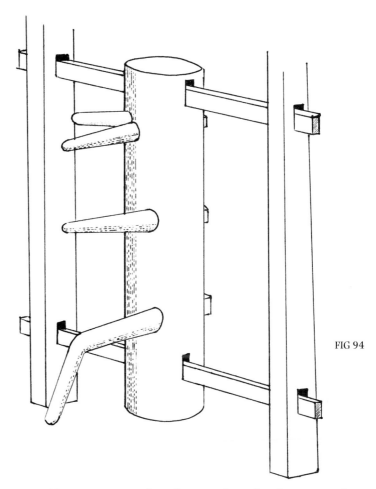

FIG 94

Wing chun kuen dummy

movement. Try to get your hands to stick to the dummy and use short-range techniques.

Practise all your techniques on the dummy, stepping around it to various angles and attempting techniques from different positions. Use single techniques at first, trying more complex double-handed sequences only when you have reached a high enough standard. Once you have learned all the techniques and how they can be used, begin fighting with the dummy as though it was a live opponent. Since your mind is no longer preoccupied with how to do the technique itself, you can forget technique and begin fighting.

After conditioning your knuckles and forearms, anoint them with tee da jao, a herb extract dissolved in alcohol. This mixture, formulated specially for wing chun kuen, contains 11 different herbs matured in alcohol for several years before use. Rubbing the extract into the knuckles gives relief from pain, keeps the joints supple, and reduces scarring. After application, leave the extract on overnight and do not wash it off. The extract forms an airtight shield over the skin, allowing the active ingredients to work.

Your teacher should be able to supply you with this most valuable training aid. If he cannot, soaking the hand and arm in hot brine will suffice, treating any bruises with a mentholated rub.

Practising basic techniques

The stance and the way in which the student holds his guard can tell the expert onlooker much about his standard. The Chinese expression for this combination of important factors is *kiu sau ma bo*. You may hold a particular stance for only an instant, but if it is unbalanced all your power and co-ordination are lost. You must therefore work hard at stances, lowering your centre of gravity while retaining your ability to move quickly in all directions.

The practice stance used for training with punches is a form of straddle posture with weight carried equally on both legs. The feet are in one line, turned in slightly, and the back is straight. Do not lean to the side, back, or front. The knees are bent forward equally. Novices often hunch their shoulders – a bad habit. Make sure your hips are thrust forwards and up, and keep your backside tucked in. This puts a strain on the leg muscles and the novice will soon find them protesting. Keep at it, though, as this is a good way to develop stability and strength.

Fighting stance uses an uneven weight distribution with around 70 per cent pressing down on the back leg. The feet are parallel and turned slightly inwards. Both lie absolutely flat on the floor (*fig 95*). The knees are bent so that they are in line with the toes. There is no fixed length for the stance; some personal variation is permitted. However, it should not be so long as to be excruciatingly uncomfortable, nor so short as to raise your centre of gravity too high.

FIG 95

56

FIG 96

To test the balance of the stance, try lifting your front foot off the ground. It should rise easily and without the need to transfer too much weight backwards. Do not be worried about having a rigid stance; if you are pushed or attacked, you can immediately turn away. Check that your back is upright, with backside tucked in. Make sure that your feet are parallel – novices tend to turn them outwards. Keep your knees bent and centre of gravity low.

There is no need to face the opponent directly from fighting stance; you can stand at an angle *(fig 96)*. Changes in angle are achieved by swivelling the hips.

FIG 97

FIG 98

The guard

A guard provides you with a means of making an effective and quick response in either attack or defence. It should not be biased in favour of either. The most basic guard is completely unspecialised. From left stance, extend your left arm until it is nearly straight, with the fingers reaching the projected centre-line of the body. Bring the right hand across and hold it with the palm facing the left elbow. Both hands are open and the fingers point slightly upwards *(fig 97)*.

An alternative guard uses two blocking arms in combination. I will deal with how these work in a later chapter; for now, simply assume the guard. If you are in right stance, raise your right arm and bring it across the front of your body. Bend it at the elbow, but not so much that the hand is turned back towards the body. Open your right hand and turn the palm so the thumb side points downwards. Now bring your left hand across, so the palm faces the right elbow and the fingers point vertically upwards *(fig 98)*. This combination of arm positions covers a large area of body and is effective against many attacks, including a straight punch *(fig 99)*.

FIG 99

You can also make an effective guard from a left stance by simply pushing one arm forwards until the elbow is only slightly bent. The hand is open, the thumb is tucked in, and the tips of the fingers are at shoulder height. Now extend your other arm forwards, so it is parallel to the first. Close your hand into a fist. The fist and open hand must not be too far apart, otherwise they will provide an opening through which an attack can come (fig 100).

This guard offers good security from attack by using body action and the open hand block to deflect strikes, yet leaving the right fist very close to the opponent where it can be used quickly. These first two stances are very good for opening free sparring, when the opponents are still a slight distance apart.

To assume yet another good guard, stand in left fighting stance and bring your left arm diagonally down across your stomach. Bend your elbow slightly and open your hand, so the fingers point forwards and the palm is turned away from the body. Your right arm is held out from the body with the palm upwards and the fingers extended into the projected centreline. Bend your elbow slightly and fold your thumb in.

FIG 100

The final stance I want to mention looks superficially similar to the last one but it is actually quite different. The right arm guards the lower body as before, but the little finger is inclined downwards. The palm of the left arm points to the side and the fingers are in the centre line of the body (fig 101). These last two stances are well suited to a close-range situation.

Bear in mind that the stance is not fixed. It represents a response to a situation; if that situation changes, the guard must change too. Therefore practise changing quickly from one stance into another, until the movement becomes automatic. A mirror will help you see any faults which may show up.

Turning from stance to stance
At some stage, you will need to turn your body suddenly by as much as 180 degrees to meet a challenge that is still distant. You must turn quickly, exchanging one stable stance for another without fumbling or losing balance or perception. This requires practice.

Start from fighting stance and step sideways with the front foot, placing it well to the front and side of the rear foot. Use your hips to twist the body with a short, sharp action. The feet rotate naturally to match the change in attitude. If you have stepped correctly, you will find you have turned on the spot and not moved body weight forward or back.

Do not draw your front foot back as you step across; if you do, you will shorten the new stance and bob up. Do step right across the front of your rear foot; if you do not, your stance will be narrow and unsteady when you turn. If, on the other hand, you step too far, you will emerge from the turn with your groin open to attack. If you remember to keep your knees bent throughout, your centre of gravity will stay low and give you stability.

As you become more proficient, combine the step across and turn into one movement. Also practise turning from one guard into another.

58

Do not use a 180 degree turn if you have an attacker standing nearby – it is too dangerous. Do not wait, but attack him from where you stand.

Moving from stance to stance

No system of Chinese martial art is ever static. You must be able to move forward to press home an attack, or move back to yield momentarily in preparation for a counter attack. Perhaps you are out of range and need to close distance, but in doing this you must keep yourself well guarded and able to respond quickly to any change in circumstances. The objective in using distance is to increase your chances of success while correspondingly diminishing your opponent's.

Wing chun kuen uses several different ways to control distance. The first and most simple way covers ground in a straight line and is called arrow walking or *jeen ma*. Use this to press home an attack or to inch forward for better range. Arrow walking, practised from fighting stance *(fig 102)*, consists of sliding the front foot forward – do not raise it clear of the ground – and drawing up the rear foot behind it *(fig 103)*. Do not move the back foot first; it is the front which initiates the step. The synchronisation of these two moves is very important because the in-between stance is vulnerable. As the front foot comes to a stop, the back foot is already moving.

FIG 101   FIG 103   FIG 102

FIG 107

When you step forward, do not lead with your chin. Your front leg moves but your body does not. Whenever you draw up your back leg, make sure it travels the correct distance. If you do not pull it far enough each time, your stance will get longer and longer. If you bring it too far forwards, your stance will get shorter and shorter. Remember to keep your back foot facing the same way and do not let it turn outwards. Maintain a constant height throughout by keeping your knees bent.

Practise arrow walking backwards as well as forwards and use various guards to gain versatility and co-ordination.

Semicircular stepping or *chum kiu ma* is the second way to move in wing chun kuen. It is used to make an attack that takes you out from the midline and in again at an angle, and it covers ground faster than jeen ma. You should practise it going backwards as well as forwards.

Keep your body back out of the way as before *(fig 104)* and maintain guard as you put weight on the front foot. Then move the back foot forwards in a shallow U which curves in towards the ankle of the leading foot *(fig 105)*. Once it passes the front foot, the leading foot swivels very slightly outwards to position it correctly for the next stance *(fig 106)*. The moving foot carries on an equal distance forwards and out, and becomes the front foot. Set it down parallel to the back foot and not skewed out.

FIG 104

FIG 105

FIG 106

Make both parts of the U step equal in length, otherwise the new stance will be too wide or too narrow, too short or too long. The supporting leg must twist slightly otherwise the change from one stance to another is ungainly. Hold your guard firmly so it does not wobble about as you step.

The most advanced movement, called *biu ma*, combines the fast forward step of *jeen ma* with the side evasion of *chum kiu ma*. Begin it with a sudden sharp move off the front leg *(fig 107, 108)*. Immediately follow this step with a semicircular step off the rear leg, like that used in *chum kiu ma (fig 109, 110)*. Synchronise the sequence of movements so the step is completed quickly. The back foot starts moving even as the front foot is completing its short step.

The same faults can occur in *biu ma* as in *jeen ma* and *chum kiu ma*, except that the sudden extension of the forward foot can make the body lean too far forward. The opening foot movement can be made in any direction. This has the effect of altering both the final length of step and the angular movement of the body. When practising *biu ma* while going backwards, step first with the back leg.

It is a good idea to combine movement with another technique, such as an attack. If you start with arrow walking from a left fighting stance, take a short step forward with the left leg and, as this step is completed, smartly bring up the back leg. Even as that is finishing, throw a strong front punch with the right hand (*fig 111*). As you punch, keep your other hand in a strong guard. If your timing is out, you will punch too early or too late. If too early, you will jar the step; if too late, you will lose the momentary advantage gained by a fast step.

Practise *biu ma* and *biu ji* together. Begin in left stance using a normal guard. Slide forwards on the left leg and bring up the right foot in a fast semicircle (*fig 112*). Maintain the guard unchanged until the right foot is about to set down in its new position, then strike out with the fingers (*fig 113*). Do not leave it too late to strike, or the energy generated by *biu ma* will be lost.

Blocking techniques

'Evil often triumphs but never conquers.'

There is nothing so boring as repeating the same simple technique over and over again. It is for this reason that I prefer modular teaching. For example, I tend not to teach a straight punch on its own but generally combine it with a block and step. This is more difficult to learn, but the student has no time to become bored – he is too busy trying to work out which bit does what and when.

Another advantage of this system is it teaches you to do several things at once. In any combat situation, it is unlikely that you will be successful responding with only one technique. You will no doubt have to respond to an attack before you can throw your punch, so it is as well if you learn how to do more than one thing at a time.

If someone throws a punch at you and you block it and then throw a counter punch, you will have lost valuable time. It would be much quicker and more effective if you blocked and punched simultaneously. Therefore practise body movement, blocking, and punching together right from the very first lesson.

At first you will be overjoyed if you can remember the sequence, let alone the precise components of the individual techniques. Do not worry if the techniques making up the sequence are not very good; this is only to be expected. The more you practise it, the less you will need to concentrate on the sequence itself and this will free your mind to concentrate on the individual moves.

Blocking theory

Wing chun kuen is characterised by economy of movement. No block or punch moves further than it needs to. Keep all your techniques, whether blocks or punches, to the centre line of the body.

The attack you face can come from varying ranges. Perhaps your opponent will stand well away and try to use kicks, or maybe he will close to where he can grasp your lapels.

There is great advantage to making an early response to an attack. As soon as your opponent moves, you must be moving too, but faster. Do not fall into the trap of looking at his fist or foot since this can be a feint. Look at his face instead, using your *ye* to determine when and where you will attack. If your *ye* is strong, it will not matter too much what attack he intends because you will be oblivious of anything except striking back. You may respond so quickly that you strike your opponent before his attack has had time to develop. After all, why should you wait to receive his kick or punch?

If you are not yet capable of making an instinctive reaction, make sure you do not let your opponent close while you are making up your mind what to do. The situation is changing constantly and any response you decide to use will be too late, simply because in the split second you conceived it, the situation will have changed. You will not know at first what form the attack is going to take so you must learn all the possibilities and select the right one unconsciously. With training, even the most complicated responses can be learned so well that they become ingrained.

Wing chun kuen uses what it calls gates to define the areas of the body. Attacks to these areas call for different responses, categorised according to the gate from which the technique comes.

If you hold your lower arms out at a right angle from the body, the space between the facing palms is the inside gate. This extends right the way down the body. Outside it is the outside gate. Above the height of the centre chest is the upper gate and from its lower margin to the waist is the lower gate. All these regions must be covered by a block of some kind.

It is never a good idea to stand your ground and block an attack. You will not know how strong your attacker is and you may misjudge his distance and angle of attack, so it is always better to evade it. A small turn away will make a technique miss yet leave you close enough to counter-attack immediately. Your stance must be strong enough to prevent you being pushed over. Typically you will not directly face your opponent but instead align your body so you are at 45 degrees to him. Bend your knees, because if you stand too high you can easily get shoved off balance. Do not stand with your knees widely separated because you can easily be kicked in the groin.

If the evasion is successful there is no need to block, though it is as well to make certain. Sometimes the attack is faster than your turn away. Even if the evasion is not wholly successful, the fact that you are turning as the blow lands may make it skid off, losing power on the way.

When you block the attack, do not waste time pushing it away. It does not matter by how much it misses, as long as it does. Practise your blocks and counters so you can use them as you are advancing, giving way, or even if you are prevented from moving at all. I advise students to start off blocking while they are stationary. Once you have got them off fairly well, try doing them on the move.

Beware of involving other parts of the body too much as this will dissipate power and make your movements too slow. Many new students try to power their blocks with strong shoulder and body action. This is not necessary. The blocking or punching arm only must be tightened, and then only in the region of the technique itself.

All blocks should be practised with a partner because this makes them realistic in application. Your partner must be someone with whom you can work co-operatively to achieve a mutual improvement. For safety's sake he should be about your size. Start with slow attacks that can easily be blocked, then, as you are able to cope, have the attacks performed faster and faster. All attacks must be on target, otherwise you will learn only how to block inaccurate ones. Sometimes this is difficult because the arms clash so heavily together that bruises develop.

Wing chun kuen blocks
The first block to be considered is *bong sau*. It is one of the safest to use because, even if the attack is strong and your turn away slow, the attack will tend to hit the blocking arm and spare the target. *Bong sau* is also a good block to start with because it is fairly forgiving. The blocking area

FIG 114

FIG 115

runs from just above the wrist on the little finger side to just below the elbow joint. This is quite an expanse of blocking surface and pinpoint accuracy is not necessary.

Bong sau is typically delivered with a rolling motion, starting from a horizontal arm held palm-up across the solar plexus. The forearm is then raised with a rolling motion, keeping the elbow close to the body. As it passes the chest, the forearm has fully rotated so the little finger edge is upwards. Use your other hand to furnish a guard *(man sau)* immediately behind your block.

Combine your blocks with concurrent attacks. In this example, I have chosen side thrust kick. The block is completed with the wrist in line with the centre of the body *(fig 114, 115)*. Do not drop or bend the wrist. The fingers must not hook and, as in all wing chun kuen open hand techniques, the thumb is hooked against the side of the hand since this tightens the wrist and makes the blocking forearm strong. It also lessens the chance of catching it in the opponent's sleeve.

Do not keep the forearm too close to the chest. Leave a margin of error by deflecting the attack while it is still some way from its target. Practising with a partner will help you to see where your block is meeting the punch. Make sure you do not block with the elbow, and do not lean forward into the block.

A powerful elbow and strong shoulder are the keys to this technique. Keep your blocking arm relaxed but not sloppy, in a state of instant readiness, and full of potential energy. As soon as it feels the attack, it should tighten up strongly. Despite this powerful contraction, the arm remains like a well tempered spring, able to bend under pressure yet spring back when pressure is eased. Do not make your arm rigid because if you do, despite all the evasions and deflections, it can break.

Continued practice of *bong sau* makes the arms feel very heavy and soon the shoulders begin to ache. This is simply because the techniques you are now practising use your muscles in a new way. To make sure you are able to block effectively, train in sticking hands.

The outside gate version of *bong sau* is particularly useful in conjunction with an evasion. Move your blocking arm as though you were doing the crawl in swimming. Let your elbow rise slightly above shoulder height and then drive it across and in front of your chest. Combine the block with a swivelling motion of the hips that turns the body first one way, then the other. The feet pivot on the heels and remain parallel.

If *bong sau* fails and collapses under a strong punch, let the arm bend but make sure you continue your twisting evasion. Allow the attack to graze your chest, using the last of its energy, then go over the top of it with a back fist.

Bong sau can be used for a variety of attacks, coming in from quite high to quite low. The edge of the hand must never rise higher than the eye line, otherwise you will not be able to see over it. At the other extreme, it can be driven downwards until the blocking forearm is almost vertical. This is useful against a low punch.

Tan sau is the next block to practise. It is a palm-up block using the area of the forearm between wrist and elbow on the thumb side. The fingers point straight and do not curl up, and the palm is in line with the forearm. Blocking action consists of a curving, rolling motion that takes the block forwards as well as out *(fig 116, 117)*. As you block, simultaneously deliver an attack such as palm heel.

FIG 116   FIG 117

You will find this combination of thrusting and rotatory motion difficult to master at first but keep at it. Do not wipe the arm across the body because this destroys the true action of the block, meeting incoming blows with a reverse chopping action instead of the thrust/deflection which is *tan sau* proper. To have maximum effect, the wrist must be strong. Keep your shoulders relaxed and do not allow them to rise up.

The completed block lies in the centre line of the body; it does not go beyond the shoulders. Any change in its orientation is accomplished by a twisting motion of the torso. The bent elbow is a fist-width away from the rib cage and the tips of the fingers come to lie just below eye level. In actual combat, however, it is permissible to extend the range of the block and the elbow can move right away from the trunk, but even then the block must be maintained in front of the shoulder. Like *bong sau, tan sau* is a safe block because it sweeps a large area and errors in accuracy will not rob it of effectiveness.

Practise *tan sau* in conjunction with a swivelling turn *(fig 118)* and make sure you keep your elbow close to the body at all times. In combat you may not have time to do other than block with a very short movement of the forearm, the turning of the body providing alignment.

Jum sau, a very powerful block, works particularly well against punches to the stomach and chest. The blocking part of the forearm is just below the elbow, on the little-finger side. The block is delivered with a cutting motion across the front of the body, the little-finger edge of the palm leading and fingers pointing *(fig 119)*.

FIG 118

FIG 119

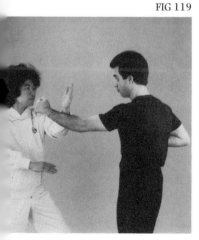

Power comes from the elbow and from the hip twist which is always associated with classic *jum sau*. As it travels forward, the blocking forearm passes close to the side of the body. The block concludes with the wrist in line with the centre of the body.

In a correct blocking action the elbow does not rise or move away from the body and the wrist does not incline ahead of the elbow; if it did, it would not sweep the attack away from the body. Always practise it with a swivelling step to the front or rear, the block completing as the step halts. If you try to block too early, your step will become jerky. If you block late, the attack may catch you.

Two common mistakes are ducking the body in behind the block and either windscreen wiping downwards with the forearm or trying to block with the elbow.

Pak sau is a slapping or pushing block which uses the palm of the hand to knock an attack off course. Since the palm of the hand is small in comparison with the length of the forearm, *pak sau* needs more skill than the blocks described earlier in this chapter. To do *pak sau* properly, you must be able to concentrate power in your wrist and lower arm, or you will never be able to knock the attack off course. Beginners tend to use *pak sau* as a push – which it is not. The blocking palm must strike the attacking technique a sharp blow.

The essence of *pak sau* lies in the concentration of localised power to produce a heavy hand. As with the punch, the lower arm must tighten up, yet the upper arm and elbow must be left free.

Pak sau can be used at various ranges, from really close in where the forearm rubs the chest *(fig 119a)*, to a long *pak sau* performed with the elbow at greater than a right angle *(fig 120)*. The latter is safer because the technique is deflected when it is well away from the body, catching the attacking elbow. The close-in version leaves little to chance because the attack has almost reached its target. *Pak sau* can also be used in the form of a descending slap that knocks the guard downwards, opening a gate through which to strike *(fig 121)*.

FIG 119A   FIG 120   FIG 121

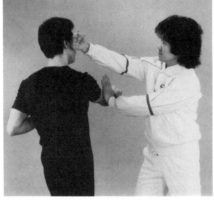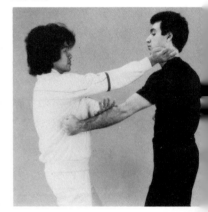

Garn sau is a lower block, effective against kicks and hooks to the ribs. Practise it in conjunction with an evasive swivelling step which takes you close to the attacker, robbing his technique of its power and target. The block begins in the centre line of the body *(fig 122, 122a)*. The arm thrusts down and rotates palm down, with deflection achieved by the little-finger side of the forearm *(fig 123, 123a)*. Because of the danger of injury, the blocking hand must be held absolutely stiff, with the thumb curled in and away from damage.

In classical *garn sau* the arm is not straight and the elbow allows it to move like a spring in compression. In practical terms, you can straighten the elbow when deflecting a really low attack.

Mistakes to avoid are swinging the blocking arm too wide of the body and bending the wrist. Do not scoop the block; make it a heavy slap that knocks the foot away. The block must be used in the manner of a deflection and not a confrontation, because in any direct contest between leg and forearm the latter always comes off worse.

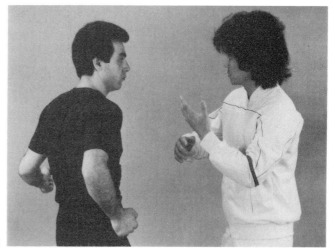

FIG 122

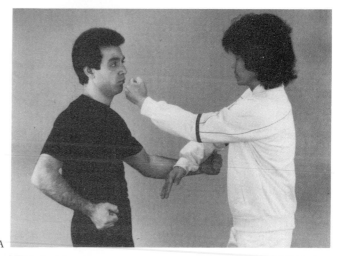

FIG 122A

FIG 123   FIG 123A

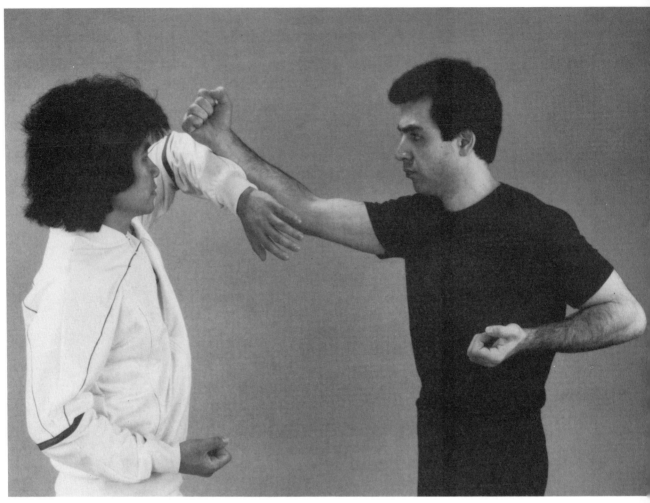

FIG 124

Gum sau, a lower deflection delivered with a slapping action like that used in *pak sau*, is not a true block but forms part of a defensive guard. It can be used very effectively to remove an obstacle to an attack, slapping it down and opening an attack path. As it thrusts down, the elbow locks; this is often used when the wrist is seized. The trapped arm is thrust into *gum sau*, breaking the grip on it. *Gum sau* can be used to the front or side.

Rising block is taught much later in the syllabus. It uses a complex curling action of the forearm to deflect a face or head attack (*fig 124*). This action is not fully comprehended by the student until he has encountered *biu je*. Until then, rising block is interpreted merely as an upward swing of the inclined forearm that both knocks the attack upwards and deflects it to one side.

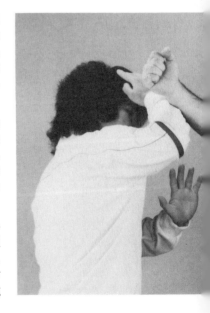

Actually the forearm travels almost vertically upwards with the little-finger edge of the hand to the side of the head. Only as it passes the head does it rotate, so the palm comes to face upwards on a slightly bent wrist. Even advanced students often take the elbow too far away from the body during the initial phases and reduce the area swept by the block. A strong

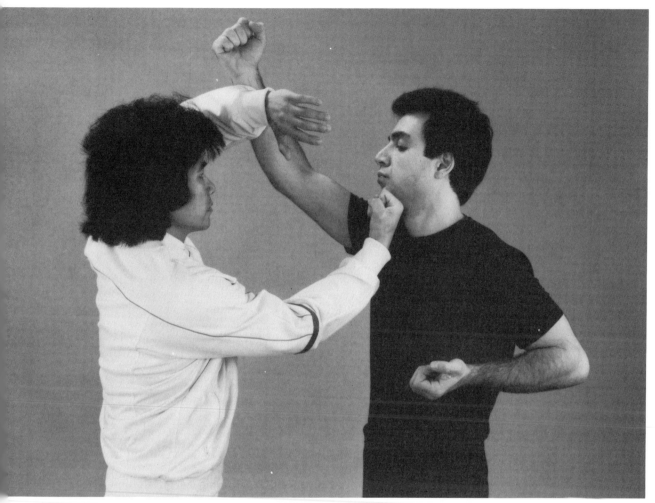

FIG 125

elbow is the key to this block, otherwise it is flabby and is easily pushed back into the head or face.

The angle of the completed rising block is very important. Whatever you do, do not hold it horizontally, lest a fierce descending blow shatter your forearm. Meet the attack at almost the same angle that it impinges on the block, so its energy is spent in a slide over the deflecting surface. If you couple angle of deflection with the rolling action of the forearm, even the hardest attack can be deflected with the minimum of force and the maximum of safety. The rising block should be coupled to an attack such as an upper cut, so the two occur simultaneously (fig 125).

I favour a simple non-traditional version of the rising block which I use when ducking to the side of a straight face attack. I throw my blocking arm up in an arc that takes the palm alongside my ear. The little-finger side of my forearm deflects the blow (fig 125a). This is very useful for deflecting short-range attacks, leaving you in close for an immediate counter.

Huen sao is a circling wrist block first encountered in the wing chun kuen pattern *siu lim tao*. You start in *jum sao* position *(fig 126)* and curl the fingers back towards your face, rotating your wrist clockwise as you see it in a full circle *(fig 127)*. Do not be tempted to cut it short. The hand rotates around an attack, controlling and deflecting it. Apply a concurrent counter attack such as a circular punch to the ribs *(fig 128)*.

Biu ji also functions as a high-level block and strike combined in one movement. Moving to the side of your opponent's attack *(fig 129)*, deflect his punch with your forearm *(fig 130)* and continue moving towards his face to deliver *biu je (fig 131)*.

FIG 126

Once you have mastered the basic blocks and can do them on the move in conjunction with a simultaneous attack, you are ready to try double blocks. These represent a tremendous safety potential because the area swept by them is so large that even if you have little idea of the nature of an attack, you are still likely to stop it. Some wing chun kuen fighting stances often use a double block as a starting point. Their use is associated with swivelling body movements.

The first double block to try is *tan sau* and a low *bong sau* in the configuration known as *kwan sau*. This is best practised with an evasion. Bring the *bong sau* up from the side, thrusting out the *tan sau* at the same time. Both arms travel in the same direction.

The beginner may find that either his *bong sau* has no rotation, catching his fingers on the attack, or his *tan sau* degenerates into a windscreen wiper.

FIG 127

Next try a combination of *jum sau* and *garn sau*, forming a composite which is also called *garn sau*. There are a couple of pitfalls to be avoided when practising this particular double block. Make sure there is no opening between your arms for an attack to slip through, and be sure to block with a strong swivelling motion of the hips. Double block on the move, using a rolling motion that allows the attack to pass by, leaving you free to spring back.

Do not block too wide with the *garn sau* or lean your body in behind the *jum sau*.

To summarise blocking theory:

1. Respond as quickly as possible to an attack.

2. Always use an evasion in conjunction with a block.

3. Never meet an attack full-on; redirect it with a glancing block.

4. Deflect an attack as far as need be and no further.

5. Use the minimum of evasion to escape. Do not move further away than you have to.

6. Use all your energy in your defence and not in a contest with the opponent's technique. Do not try to stop him.

7. Make sure you are well balanced, or you may be driven back or pushed over.

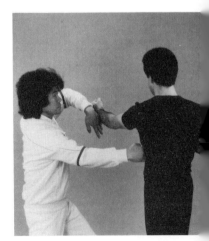

FIG 128

FIG 129

FIG 130

FIG 131

Sticking hand practice

'Be yourself. Who else is better qualified?'

Sticking hands is an ingenious form of training which reaches its highest state of development only in wing chun kuen. In Cantonese it is called *chi sau, poon sau* ('rolling hands'), or *go sau* ('passing hands') to describe the nature of the practice – to keep your arms in constant contact with your opponent's. In essence, sticking hands teaches you how to cope with and succeed in the hurly-burly of a close-range confrontation. It also strengthens the body and widens perception.

If you have ever seen a real fight, you will know that the combatants do not stand at an elegant distance and fight cleanly. Usually they close in and try to grab, trip, or push. You must be able to withstand such tactics and turn them to your advantage. That is the purpose of sticking hands. Its very name tells you that it is a close-range activity, practised from literally only an arm's length.

To gain all the advantages afforded by sticking hands, you must close in on the opponent. At such range your techniques will remain effective while his are blocked by your very closeness. There are not many styles teaching techniques that are effective at arm's length or less. Fighting from such close range has some fairly obvious disadvantages for less skilled people. Each punch or strike has to travel only a very short distance to its target; in consequence, counter-attacks must be almost instantaneous – there is no room for mistake or delay. To cope with this, sticking hands practice is structured in such a way that you can set up conditioned

74

reflexes which allow automatic response.

There is much to-ing and fro-ing in sticking hands and experienced students apply a constant pressure to their partner's forearms in an effort to test the resilience of a certain move. This can provide clues to any weak areas to be exploited. You can also use this pressure to guide the opponent's guard into an unfavourable position, creating an opening for your attack. All the pressure is applied with raised arms, so aches and pains during early days of practice are common. Not only must your arms be strong but your stance must be too, and this means keeping your knees bent. As soon as you straighten them you can be pushed off balance.

Do not fight the opponent's strength, but save your energy to attack him. Keep your arms in close contact all the time, even when he is circling you or moving about. If your arm movements are stiff, they will become jerky and lose contact with his. If they are flabby and loose, he will be able to force through them and attack you directly. Try to function like a spring, yielding but not falling away. Let your opponent's strength push your arm back but turn it to your advantage by releasing the tension built up in it with an attack.

Single sticking hand techniques

The basic exercise to start practising sticking hands uses a simple combination of techniques performed on one side only. At first both partners stand still, so all you have to do is concentrate on the movement of your arm. Hold the left hand lightly against the ribs with fist closed and palm facing upwards. Stand in straddle stance facing your partner and check range by extending your hand and touching his shoulder.

FIG 132

Punch to his mid chest with your right hand. He deflects the punch upwards using a left hand *bong sau* block *(fig 132)*. After he blocks your punch, let it rest on top of his forearm.

Your partner changes to *tan sau* by dropping his left elbow straight down; it must not curve outwards as it does. Because your punch is resting on his arm, as he drops his arm you will automatically follow, opening your fingers and rotating palm down into *fook sau (fig 133)*. It overlies the opponent's lower forearm and rests on it.

FIG 133

From *tan sau*, your partner tries to make a palm heel strike to your chest but your *fook sau* detects the movement as it begins and deflects the thrust harmlessly downwards *(fig 134)*. This deflection uses a crisp action of the wrist; it is not merely a downwards push. Point your fingers vertically upwards and concentrate power into the thrust. Having knocked your partner's arm down, bring your right hand smartly up and try to punch him in the chest. If his guard is resilient, he will keep contact with your forearm and deflect the punch upwards as he uses *bong sau* once again. At this point, the sequence is ready to begin again.

When you exchange roles, remember to drop your elbow vertically from *bong sau* into *tan sau*. Do not forget to make *tan sau* lower than *bong sau* and pay close attention to the position of your elbow, which should remain a constant distance from the body. Thrust straight at your partner's chest from *tan sau* and he will immediately deflect your arm downwards. His

FIG 134

arm will then rise quickly so make sure you keep contact with it, changing to a *bong sau* as you do. If his punch is sharp you may find your *bong sau* rising too high. Avoid this bad mistake.

When you can do this basic sequence reasonably well, try it using the opposite arms. You must be ambidextrous in sticking hands or you will lose 50 per cent of your capability. When you can do the sequence with either hand, begin moving around so as to add another order of complexity. Now you must not only concentrate on faithfully following the movements of your partner's arm, but you will have to keep pace with him as he changes position.

The second single hand sequence uses a right *bong sau* block to stop a back fist to the face. Guard with *man sau* held close behind the *bong sau* (fig 135) and, with a short action, reach up and grasp the back fist with it, using wrist action only. The little finger curls around first, followed by the others. Do not raise your elbow to the side. Pull your partner's arm down and to one side, freeing your *bong sau* (fig 136) so it can spring into a back fist to his face (fig 137). This drawing action is a continuous movement called *lap sau*. Your partner deflects the back fist using *bong sau* delivered with his left arm. Reaching forward with his guarding *man sau*, he grasps your back fist and pulls it to one side and down, so he can strike you with back fist, whereupon the sequence begins again.

FIG 135

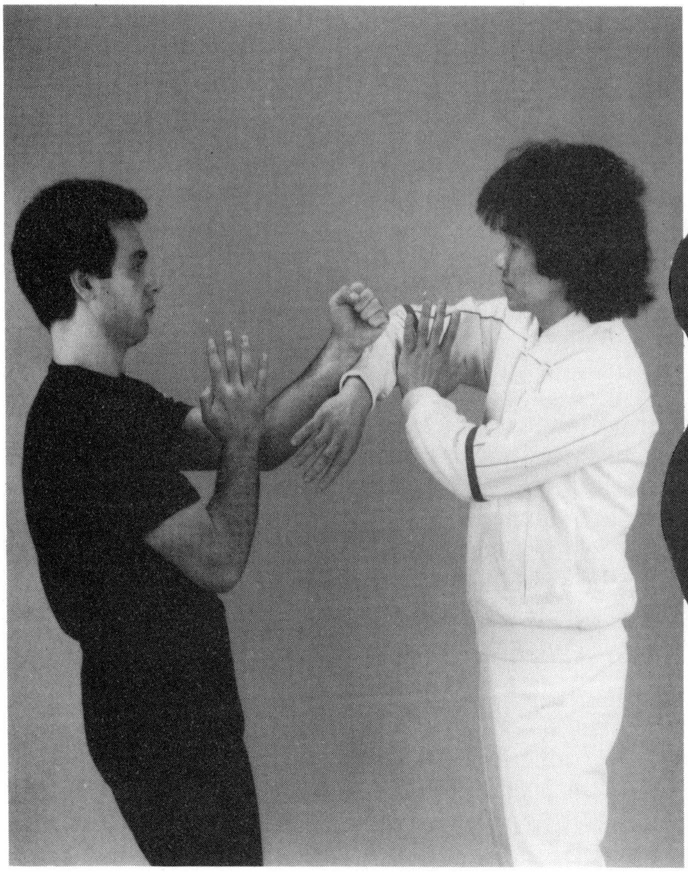

FIG 136

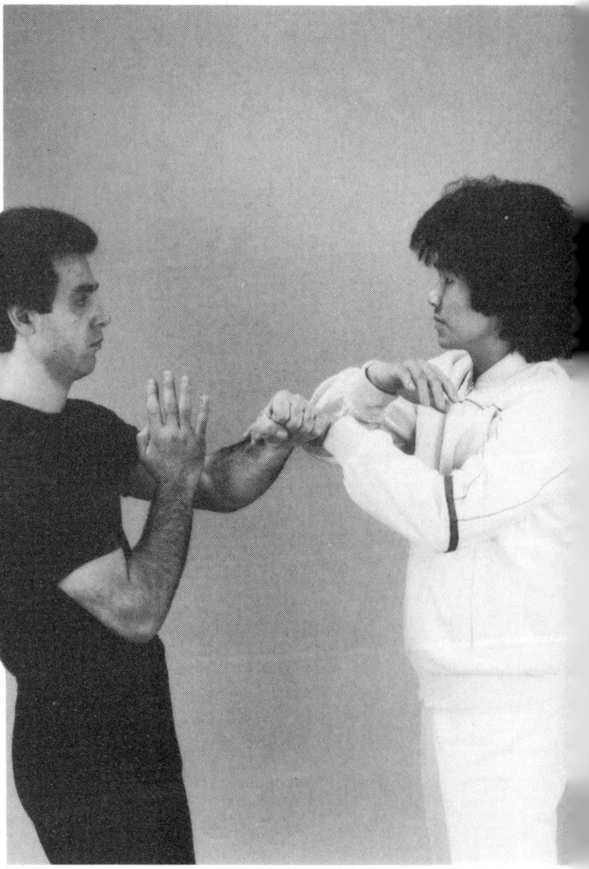

When you grasp his back fist and pull it down, do not pull it too far but only enough to free your *bong sau*. Do not twist his arm, and release it immediately his *man sau* touches your back fist.

Train with both hands, suddenly changing them over without interrupting the smooth flow of movement. If your opponent is following you closely, he will detect the change immediately it happens and make the appropriate response. As he tries to draw your back fist down, resist. He will feel this resistance and release his grasp, whereupon you strike with a second back fist, this time using your other hand. He immediately responds with *bong sau* on his opposite arm and the cycle begins again.

FIG 137

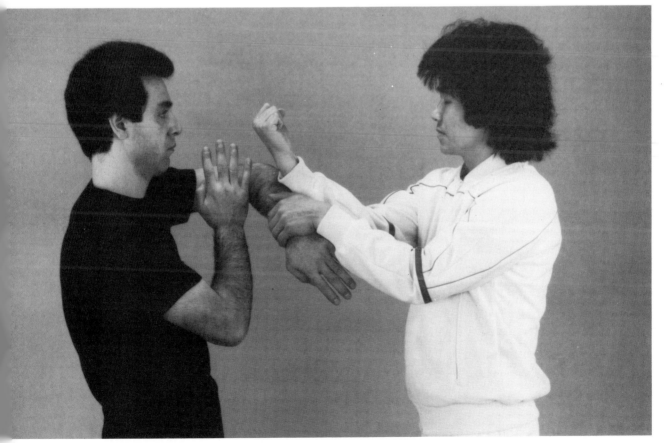

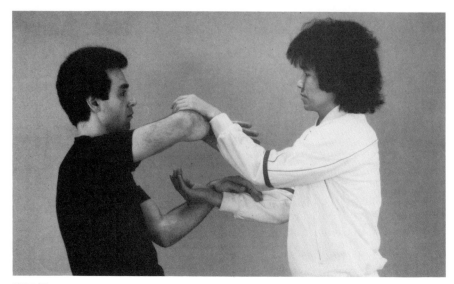

FIG 138

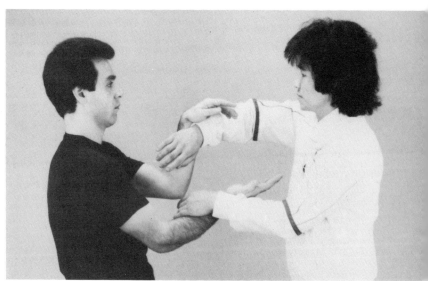

FIG 139

Double sticking hand techniques

Double sticking hand techniques are confusing to learn at first but are soon picked up. Each person uses two hand positions alternatively. In the first position, he may use a right *bong sau* and a low left *fook sau*. In the second position, the *bong sau* has dropped sharply to become right *tan sau*, and low *fook sau* changes to a high one. Your opponent also uses a right *bong sau* dropping to *tan sau*, plus lower and upper left *fook sau*.

Curl your left high *fook sau* over his *bong sau*; hold your *tan sau* out and his lower *fook sau* will rest on it *(fig 138)*. Move your lower *tan sau* sharply upwards into *bong sau*, and his *fook sau* will move with it. At the same time, he drops his right *bong sau* into *tan sau* and your high *fook sau* follows it down *(fig 139)*. Your left hand just lies on his right arm. Keep both *fook sau* well clear of the body. As your arms rise, exert a slight pressure against your opponent's forearms. Very soon a rhythmic synchronised sequence

FIG 140   FIG 140A

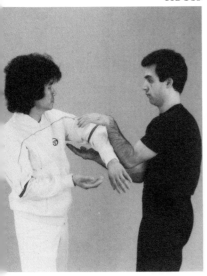
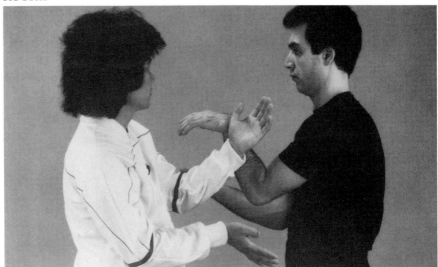

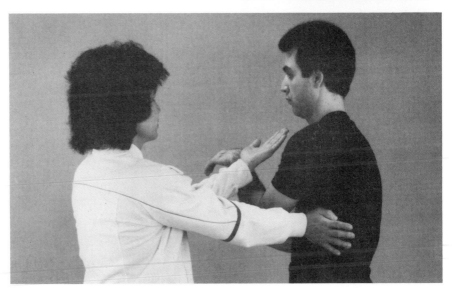

FIG 141

is established, with elbows pumping up and down as cycle follows cycle. This is the foundation from which double sticking hand techniques are built.

While both partners keep perfect form, the opportunities for a successful attack are small. Eventually, however, one of them makes a small mistake and the other seizes on it. For example, if you raise and lower your arms at a slight angle, your opponent's arms will cross, providing you with an opening. As you drop your *bong sau* drive it between his arms *(fig 140)*, so when you change it to *tan sau*, you end up knocking both his arms away to the side *(fig 140a)*. Your left hand drops away from *fook sau* and strikes him in the ribs with palm heel *(fig 141)*. This action is smooth and uninterrupted from start to finish. If you hesitate or signal your intention, your opponent will detect it and counter.

At any time when you are doing *bong sau (fig 142)* you can suddenly twist your hips and bend your elbow past your opponent's upper *fook sau*. As you are changing from *bong sau* to *tan sau*, drop your right hand down and seize his right *tan sau*, trapping his left arm against his body with the back of your elbow *(fig 143)*. At the same time, your lower *fook sau* pulls clear of his *tan sau* and when your hips finish twisting you are close enough to punch to his face with your left hand *(fig 144)*.

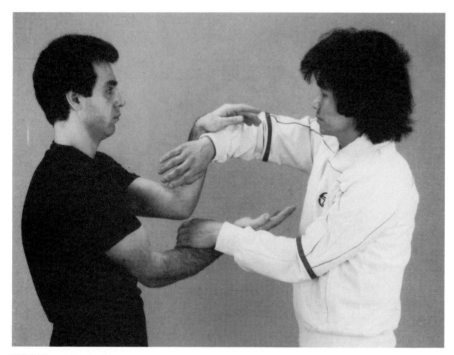

FIG 142

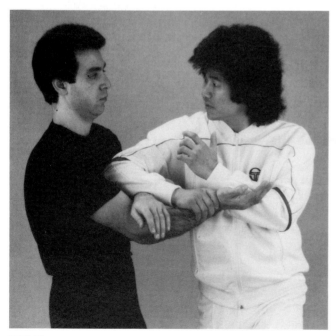

FIG 143

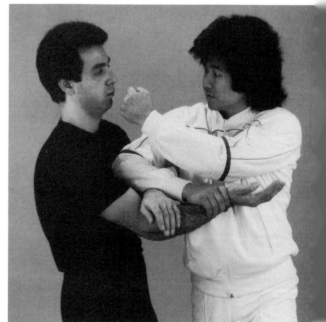

FIG 144

As the corollary of the last technique, you can attack as you drop from the high *fook sau* position *(fig 145)* by quickly sliding your left hand over the top of your opponent's *bong sau* and hooking it downwards so it seizes his left elbow in an overarm grasp using pushing block, or *boot sau (fig 146)*. Move slightly to the right as you go for the grasp and scoop his left arm out of the way, bringing your right fist round in a circling punch to his ribs *(fig 147)*.

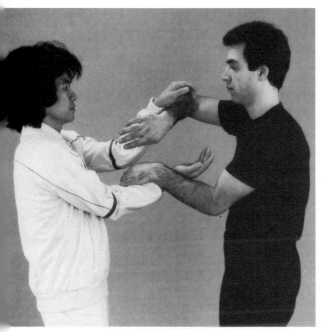

FIG 145

FIG 146

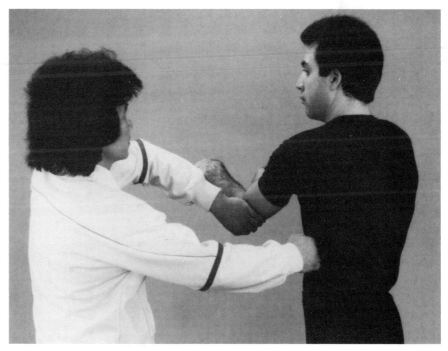

FIG 147

You can also attack from lower *fook sau (fig 148)* by sharply lifting the hand up and smacking *pak sau* into the side of your opponent's high *fook sau (fig 149)*. Your forearm bars his *tan sau* from further involvement and your *bong sau* is freed to cut directly up into the side of his neck with a chop *(fig 150)*.

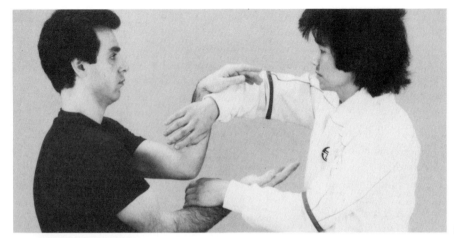

FIG 148

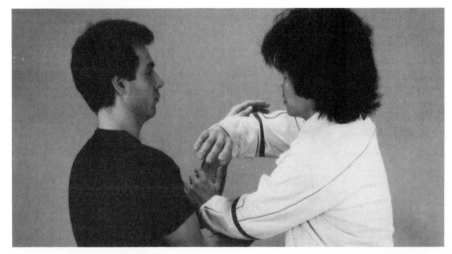

FIG 149

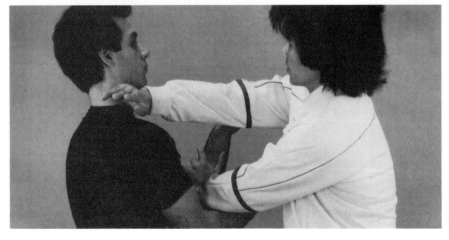

FIG 150

A second sequence from lower *fook sau (fig 151)* attacks his left arm as before, but instead of just doing *pak sau*, the fingers close around his forearm and pull his *fook sau* clear of your *bong sau*. Your left forearm bars across both of his *(fig 152)* and you strike upwards with right palm heel into his jaw *(fig 153)*.

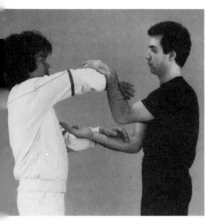
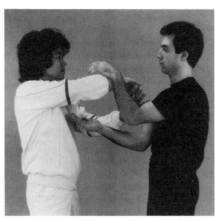
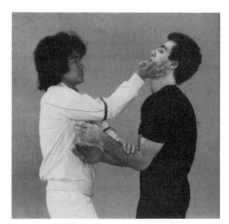

FIG 151   FIG 152   FIG 153

The final sequence attacks both your opponent's arms simultaneously as they reach the same height during the sequence. Grasp his lower *fook sau* with your right *tan sau* and pull his *bong sau* with your *fook sau (fig 154)*. Then bring your right foot up and kick him in the lower stomach or groin with the flat of your foot *(fig 155)*.

FIG 154   FIG 155

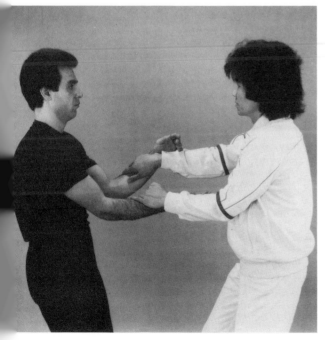

83

Free sparring

A prime tenet of wing chun kuen can be expressed as 'Use minimum effort to achieve maximum effect'. This economical approach fits in well with the highest principles of free sparring, regardless of the school. When you watch two people spar, count the number of times an attack fails through missing the target or being blocked. You will see students using techniques like machine guns, firing off whole salvoes of them in the hope that one will hit home. By way of contrast, the master will use very few carefully chosen techniques but each one will hit the target.

Free sparring at any level in wing chun kuen can be hazardous. For that reason I recommend that you do not try it until you have reached a good standard of practice. After all, if you cannot block well, you should not get into a position where you have to block in order to escape injury.

When you block or punch, you must be able to develop power only in the weapon you are using and not implicate other parts of the body lest you slow your reactions and make techniques ineffective. Instead, try to keep relaxed except for localised force in the technique you are using. If you cannot do this properly, you may suffer injury through, for example, wrist flexing on impact. Control is also needed for your opponent's safety. Your mastery of technique must be such that you can hit safely, fast, and on target, yet with a calculated degree of impact that stops short of causing your opponent injury.

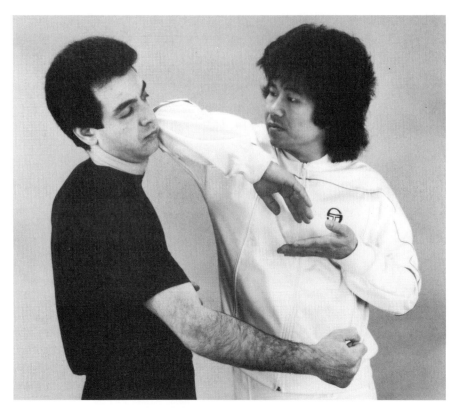

Close range effectiveness is essential

Turn every situation to your advantage

Exercise care attacking vulnerable targets

People sometimes ask why I do not use body armour or protective equipment, such as a head guard. The reason is that wearing it significantly alters response to an attack. You grow to rely on the protection afforded by armour and this makes you lazy. It even affects your movements; for example, heavy head armour slows the way you would normally use your upper body. You can use a very light sleeveless jacket braced with glass fibre or bamboo, but I find it cumbersome and uncomfortable.

I do, however, recommend wearing thinly padded protective mitts, but for the sake of the opponent, not the user. The mitts must allow you to open your hand fully and they must not restrict the action of the thumb. Some mitts have a padded thumb, but this stops you from making a good fist and the semi-closed thumb can catch in clothing.

When you begin sparring, try to get your partner to co-operate for your mutual benefit. Set a level of speed and power which allows you both to cope without getting injured. If your partner is much better than you, he can destroy your confidence by easily defeating your best efforts while giving you a hiding.

If your partner wants to help you, he will adapt the complexity and tempo of his actions to match yours, but this certainly does not mean going easy on you. A periodic pointed exposition of your weaknesses is better than a thousand words of advice. As abilities improve, so speed can increase, but even when you are both going at it hammer and tongs, you must control your impact. If you fail, a mistake can prove very painful.

Control of distance is the first step towards doing well in free sparring. As you know, wing chun kuen works very well at short distances, where there is little time to correct a mistake or formulate a response. The correct distance for wing chun kuen sparring is literally an arm's length from your opponent. This makes every punch or strike in range and likely to hit home unless it is stopped.

If you stand at a distance greater than arm's length, you will not be able to reach your opponent except through a lengthening of stance, a closing step, or some other mechanism to get into striking range. If you learn only how to block attacks which signal themselves through a run-up of some kind, you will always be too slow for wing chun kuen.

Block all attacks from actual fighting range and do not rely on steps, shifts of balance, or other signals that an attack is about to be launched. Even during basic blocking practice your partner should give no warning when he is about to strike. If he does, you will never generate the awareness needed to be effective at close distances. You may have a powerful block, but is it fast enough? Only a proper evaluation in a realistic situation can answer that question.

Some martial artists prefer to fight from middle to long distances, suddenly diving in and using extended hand strikes and kicks. If you try to fight on their terms, you will probably lose. Your wing chun kuen techniques will not be so effective at long range and all you can do is block. You must jam in close because long hand forms are at a tremendous disadvantage when crowded, since all their techniques are designed for a different application.

At greater distances, use kicks

If you jam in close you can unbalance your opponent, at which point he loses all possiblity of effective counter-attack. Naturally, he will not care too much for these tactics and will keep trying to pull back, so you must keep crowding in close. Whatever you do, do not allow him to pull away or you will be back to square one.

Additionally, closing with someone robs him of any physical advantage he may have. For example, a long reach favours middle- to long-range combat, but if you get inside it, it becomes a positive disadvantage. Once jammed in, you can use short-range attacks such as palm heel to the face. In these circumstances I never recommend using a knee into the groin because when you are that close, standing on one leg – for however short a time – is dangerous. In a real fight, your attacker will not stand by while you tee him up for a technique. He will be flailing, pushing, and shoving with such vigour that standing on one leg is definitely not to be recommended.

The tactical fighter can make use of angle of attack to ensure that his techniques are favoured at the expense of his opponent's. *Chum kiu ma* and *biu ma* take you quickly into a position where you can attack the opponent through his inside or outside gate. If you are strong, move to his outside gate. From this position, his possibilities for immediate attack are reduced while yours are great.

If you are not so strong, he can push you away. Stepping through into the inside gate carries risks because you are moving into an area where he can

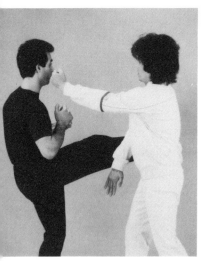

Attack him as he attacks you

Attack and defend simultaneously

use as many techniques as you can, but if it is done skilfully, initiative remains with the attacker. This tactic is more suited to the less strong person.

Another principle of successful free sparring is timing – knowing when to act and, conversely, when not to. If you react too slowly, you will be hit. You must be able to detect your opponent's *ye* so you can catch him as he is attacking. Do not wait until the attack is almost on you before you react. Strike him as he begins his attack, eschewing a block in favour of a technique which closes his off while leaving yours with a clear field.

You must develop a wide range of techniques if you want to be successful at free sparring. Over-reliance on favourite techniques soon gets noticed and countered, leaving you with little chance of victory. Make sure you are versatile and able to attack or defend with equal ability. If you prefer attacking to defending, concentrate on and build up your defence, and vice versa.

You may notice that your opponent prefers always to be on the attack. If so you may find his defence not so strong, so attack him strongly and keep him under pressure. Perhaps your opponent does nothing except wait for you to attack and, when you do, he counter-attacks. This could mean that he prefers defence to offence and therefore you should draw him out and make him come to you.

Look for weaknesses in the opponent. These are visible to the skilled martial artist through assessment of the stance and guard. The way he moves will tell you much about his ability and demeanour. Remember that he is testing you too, so avoid giving clues.

Put your hand out well towards him and see what he does. By contacting his leading hand you may be able to tell whether he is stiff and likely to move slowly, or resilient and likely to snap back as soon as you put him under pressure. The stiff fighter will be unable to turn quickly to meet an attack from a different angle. If he manages to grab you, do not fight his grip. Instead move with it, using his strength to your advantage.

Treat every move from the opponent as a serious threat and make no distinction between feints and actual attacks. If you can free spar properly, then even though the opponent may only be feinting, you have reacted before his follow-up can be launched. If you are fast enough, you will be able to retaliate even before he has finished the feint.

One of the worst things is to hit someone who does not go down. When this happens you must have a fusillade of techniques ready to follow each other with such speed that they wear the opponent down through accumulated damage.

When your free sparring is very well developed, then by all means try sparring with students from other schools. Provided you do so in a spirit of mutual respect and without ego or malice, you will learn a great deal from each other. Remember, though, you cannot pit two styles against each other; you can only pit people. A bad performance does not necessarily reflect discredit on the loser's style.

Self defence

You may be the biggest and strongest person in the world but, through fear, you still may not be able to defend yourself against even the smallest assailant. If you can overcome fear, you can defend yourself. The practical techniques you use are of less importance.

Fear stems from insecurity. You are afraid only because you are unaware of your own ability. The opponent may be much larger and stronger than you are, but these are not the only ingredients needed to win. Will-power and speed are also important and they are not the prerogatives of the large and hairy. Though your opponent may be larger than you, he can never know for certain he will win.

Not all big people are as tough as you might think. Some are physically strong but mentally weak and this turns them into bullies and cowards. They are insecure and therefore feel fear. The show-off martial artist may break a brick by way of demonstration but the first time it does not break and injures him, he is frightened for the rest of his life. The coward will try to avoid getting into a position of challenge in case he fails. His fragile ego will not take kindly to failure.

Martial art training is all about challenges. You are challenged to reach and go through your own limits of endurance and capability; your hardest taskmaster is yourself, not the teacher. You find yourself and develop *ye*, the will to act, through taking up this challenge and defeating yourself.

Through training you become aware of yourself and your capability and this leads to a loss of fear.

The *ye* is limitless. A child is born without ideas of weakness or relative strength; his is the simple will to act. Do not consider *ye* as a conscious or reasoning force because it is not. You cannot consciously think yourself into becoming tough. You cannot fake *ye*; if you pretend, you will soon be found out.

Some small people are naturally assertive, with an aura of capability and determination that belies their small stature. Such people are less likely to be attacked.

The martial artist will try to avoid trouble; if he stoops to needless violence he is no better than his attacker. If you study wing chun kuen hard, you will develop the ability to inflict injury or pain and so you must be careful. If someone is rude to you, that is his problem, not yours. Ignore him and do not let yourself become angry. Anger destroys inner calmness and will impair any physical response you may have to make.

Fighting is uncontrolled agression. Anybody can fight without knowing self defence. On the other hand, the essence of self defence is controlled agression. Fighting involves a great deal of wasteful violence while self defence uses controlled violence to a purpose. If you are certain that an attack is imminent, there is no need to wait. Attack the aggressor first with a warning shot that causes a deal of pain but minimal injury. Pain is the key to effective self defence; if you inflict enough, the attacker will withdraw.

Someone high on drugs has a raised pain threshold and you may have to hit him several times before physical damage brings him to a halt. Several punches landing on the same spot can have a cumulative effect, the first perhaps breaking the skin and the others worsening the damage. The result is to slow the attacker down, so his techniques lose their force and speed.

Avoiding trouble

Today's world is a violent one but it is possible to avoid trouble by observing a few common-sense safeguards. Do not walk around with your head in the clouds. Be aware of what is happening around you and you may be able to head trouble off. If your mind is still, it is receptive to stimulus. The car driver who is concentrating on his dinner fails to see the car stop in front of him.

The first line of self defence is your natural awareness, which comes through training. If you have to concentrate all the time on what is happening around you, your mind will eventually become tired and you will begin to miss things. Natural awareness requires no energy to maintain it.

We hear many hints about where to walk and how not to dress at night but I always think these are unrealistic. We have not yet reached the stage where we have to behave as though everyone we meet is a potential mugger. Rather than constructing an elaborate series of safeguards that are difficult to sustain, become proficient in your study of martial art. Use your awareness to avoid trouble but do not start at shadows.

I am very sceptical about so-called self-defence courses because I do not think anyone can learn enough in so short a time. The techniques shown are often excellent, but without the will power to perform them, they cannot work. Some of them are very complicated to operate and I am not sure that the untrained person can be sufficiently cool under pressure to apply them properly.

So far as I am concerned, the only way to learn effective self defence is to pick a martial art and train hard in it until its techniques are second nature to you. It is to be hoped the art you select will include the most important ingredient in successful self defence – training you to have control over your fear.

Some physical self-defence techniques
The physical actions of self defence are unimportant; you can draw from any of the wing chun kuen techniques shown in this book.

FIG 156

FIG 157

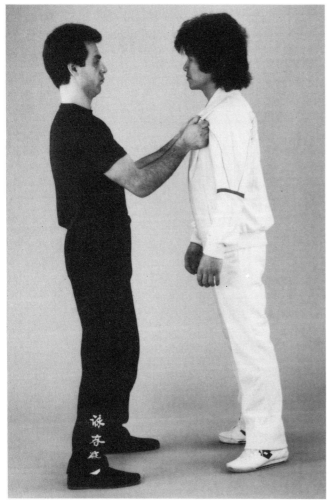

For the sake of argument, let us assume that despite all your training you have failed to take the initiative and the attacker has managed to grab hold of you. For the first technique I have selected a double lapel grab (*fig 156*). Although commonplace, it is a particularly stupid way to start an attack because the assailant has used his two most versatile weapons to hold my jacket. That leaves him with only his head and knees to use.

The last thing I intend to do is stand there while the attacker shakes me about like a rag doll. If he pulls me forward, I will operate standard wing chun kuen theory and instead of resisting the pull – squandering all my energy fighting his attack – I will go with him and maybe knee him in the groin or thigh. Otherwise I will step back sharply (*fig 157*) and drive my extended fingers into his throat (*fig 158, 159*). A hard thrust from stiffened fingers will cause him to release his grasp.

When you strike upwards, keep your elbow close to your body and do not take your eyes off the attacker's face. Do not leave him holding on to your lapels for too long; you must take the initiative from him.

FIG 158   FIG 159

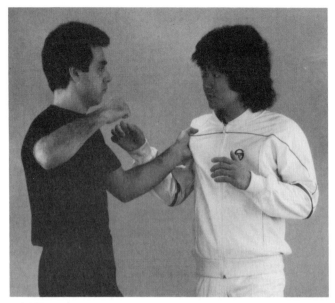

FIG 160

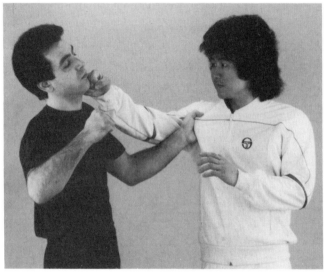

FIG 161

FIG 162

In the second sequence, the attacker has grabbed my lapel with one hand and is threatening to punch me *(fig 160)*. I choose not to wait for him to throw his punch but react immediately by getting in first *(fig 161)*. It is important to act immediately. In grabbing your lapel he has shown actual physical aggression and you need not delay an appropriate response.

In the third sequence, I have been caught with a throat bar from behind *(fig 162)*. This is a nasty technique because it stops you breathing, reduces blood supply to the brain, or both. If it stops you breathing, you will immediately begin panicking and your movements will become diffuse and unfocused. If it cuts down blood supply, you will gradually lose consciousness. As soon as this technique is applied, you must act fast.

FIG 163

FIG 164

I have seen some techniques where the victim stamps on the attacker's toes or elbows him in the ribs. I do not think either of these will work in a real situation. You cannot see his feet so you end up stamping ineffectually while your consciousness fades. Not many people can deliver an effective elbow strike while they are being throttled. My advice is to aim for a sensitive target such as the groin.

A sharp hammer fist back into the attacker's groin will provoke a swift reaction, even if it misses the testicles *(fig 163)*. If you catch them, all well and good, but even if you miss, the effect of your blow will be to loosen his grip and bring his head forwards. Strike over your shoulder with the tips of your fingers and the chances are that you will catch his eyes *(fig 164)*.

In the last sequence I have allowed myself to be grabbed by the wrist (*fig 165*). Again the important thing is not to fight the grab. Concentrate your energy on your response, not on competing with the attacker's strength. If he drags you forwards (*fig 166*), so much the better. Go with him and take a big step to help you on your way. Let the elbow he has grasped bend, and thump him in the chest (*fig 167*). Provided your sudden forward step is quick enough, he will not be able to stop pulling you in time and you may find that he has lost his balance.

As soon as I barge the attacker, I immediately bring up my free hand and deliver a knife hand to his throat (*fig 168*). I do not need a special stance because I have trained to make my hand very heavy. When it strikes his throat, he will release my hand.

Once I step back a little, I can either run away or continue with an attack. It depends on how the attacker will react when he gets to his feet. If you think he is sufficiently discouraged by what you have done, leave it at that. If, on the other hand, you feel he is likely to offer more violence, then

FIG 165

FIG 166

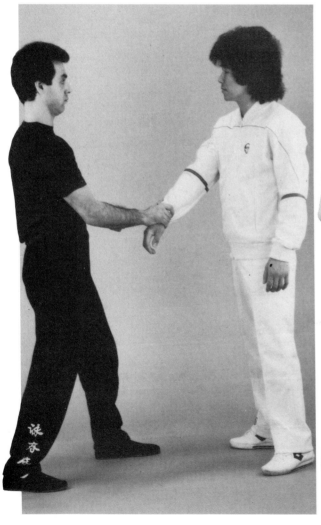

you should use the opportunity to deal him enough physical punishment to dissuade him without allowing him to regain the initiative.

Please do not over-react but apply your techniques carefully. All you want to do is to stop him attacking you but to cause him the least possible damage. Avoid dangerous techniques in favour of painful deterrents. My own favourite is a one-knuckle fist into the shoulder which causes a great deal of pain but little actual injury. If this is properly applied, the attacker will not be able to lift his arm for several minutes after the strike. A knee strike to his thigh will also cause pain but not injury.

If your attacker produces a weapon, you can be a little more forceful in the techniques you use, because if you fail there is a likelihood of your sustaining real injury.

In conclusion, let me stress again that wing chun kuen is a fighting system and all its techniques are applicable to self defence. The most important aspect of self defence, however, is your will.

FIG 167

FIG 168

The philosophy of fitness

'*Art is the opening of all human capacities –
thought, feeling and will. Artistic skill does not
mean artistic perfection.*'

This chapter is all about being healthy, but you will not find many references to press-ups and knee-bends. Health is often confused with fitness, and many people think that if you are fit you must be healthy. Such is not the case.

One of the drawbacks of fitness training is that it can unbalance the body. We all have a natural level of health which allows us to perform normal everyday tasks; we say we are fit to do them. If we decide we want to be fit to perform tasks which are not normal, then we step on a slippery slope.

Let us say that you are a civil servant. Provided you take care not to damage your health too badly, you will be fit enough to do your job and still have enough left over to bound up a flight of stairs or take the dog for a long hike across the fells. It could be, though, that you want to lift enormous weights in your spare time, so you decide to increase your fitness.

Every night you get on the exercise machines and pump iron until your damaged muscles respond by increasing their efficiency and bulk. While you are hard at work weight-lifting all will be well, but as soon as you pack it in, your bulging muscles quickly turn to fat and your hard-won fitness vanishes. An artificial level of heightened fitness is very hard work to maintain throughout a lifetime, so think carefully before you decide to become super-fit.

To be healthy, your whole body must work efficiently. The heart must pump blood around the body in sufficient volumes, the viscera must efficiently convert food into metabolites, and the kidneys must filter waste. Whatever exercises we decide to do must stimulate our body to perform these functions as efficiently as possible.

Health through bodily harmony

Since this is a book about an eastern martial art, it is appropriate for me to describe the ancient health principles practised by the masters. They believe that the functions of the body interact in a dynamic way; when one function increases, another correspondingly decreases. This is also a very modern principle of western medicine – homeostasis, which is known to be responsible for such processes as the menstrual cycle.

In Taoist philosophy the two fundamental essences of the living body are *yum* and *yeung* (*yin* and *yang* in Mandarin). *Yum* is normally associated with the female essence and *yeung* with the male. The living body contains both and, at times, one or the other will be predominant. The balance between them is a delicate one which can be affected by many different factors. For example, if you eat a hot curry *yeung* increases and can be countered only by an intake of some *yum*-rich food such as lager. The whole edifice of health rests on maintaining this balance. *Yum* is associated with water, earth, and things above ground; *yeung* is associated with air, fire, and things below ground. A potato will be rich in *yum*; chillis and peanuts are examples of things rich in *yeung*. If you keep the balance with a sensible diet, you will be well on your way towards better health.

When *yum* and *ying* are in their normal range of equilibrium, the body produces an energy which all living things possess. Chinese call this naturally occurring energy *jing*. It is abundant in young, undamaged, growing things. Children have it in great quantities and that is why they seem tireless in comparison with most of us. Their young bodies are relatively unharmed by unhealthy habits of adult life and the *jing* flows freely through them. Their inexhaustible energy is not the result of special training, but a natural consequence of their health.

Jing is produced in three regions of the body: head, spine, and viscera. The Chinese call them *ye, jong chih,* and *dan tien* respectively. All three centres must generate *jing* if boundless energy is to result. Academicians often produce a preponderance of *jing* energy from the head, making them fast thinkers but not necessarily very physically active. In contrast, athletes produce a lot of *jing* energy from their spinal regions. People whose *jing* energy is over-produced in the viscera suffer from physical sexual failures triggered by over-excitability.

To achieve a balanced production of *jing* in all three centres, you should follow a simple excercise programme allied with breathing techniques described later in this chapter.

Chi is a universal force which pervades the whole universe. A person whose *jing* energy is in balance can draw *chi* energy from his surroundings and concentrate it within his body. Once there, it flows around the body in precise channels called meridians. *Chi* augments the natural energy of the body and can help the person who possesses it to perform feats of amazing stability and strength.

By pressure, needles, or medicines, the flow of *chi* along a particular meridian can be influenced and can produce spectacular results. The real reason for wearing a sash is not, as you might imagine, to denote rank; it is used in the manner of a bodybuilder's belt, to hold the *chi* in the body and stop it diffusing.

Your diet

Diet is an important ingredient of both health and fitness. You are what you eat, no less. To achieve maximum health you must eat regularly and ensure a balance between carbohydrates, fats, and proteins. Carbohydrates produce energy and provide fuel for training. The muscles need the carbohydrate glucose to produce contraction and the body contains a chemical factory which can split any carbohydrate you eat down to this simple sugar or its twin, fructose. Carbohydrates surplus to your body's requirements are converted and stored as fat.

Fats are efficient means of long-term energy storage but they cannot be broken down quickly enough to provide an immediate replenishment for carbohydrates used during exertion. The body needs to take in very little fat; most of us eat far too much of it. Surplus fat produces unsightly bags of flesh and many people cannot remove it from the bloodstream where it clogs up the vessels.

Protein is the body-builder. During the process of living, bits and pieces wear out and have to be replaced. The body takes in protein and chops it up into its component amino acid sub-units, rejoining them in a particular way to produce new body tissue. Excess protein is broken down and got rid of through the kidneys.

In addition to these substances, the body needs various minerals and complicated substances known as vitamins. These can be bought in bottles but in the eastern view such preparations are dead and of limited value. It is far better to eat an orange than to swallow a vitamin C pill. For this reason, all your food must be fresh. That which is long dead or preserved has lost the residual life energy it once held.

Too much of the fresh food we eat has been refined and has lost its goodness. Try to eat wholefoods whenever possible. Brown rice is better than white rice; wholemeal bread is better than white bread. Roughage is an important part of our food and if we do not get enough, constipation and bowel problems quickly set in.

Fluids are vital, especially when you consider that the body is 94 per cent water. Remember your *yum* and *yeung* balance and drink enough to maintain it. Not unnaturally, I recommend Chinese tea as a good way of taking fluid. The infusion of herbs produces a drink which can dissolve fats very quickly. Chinese tea also helps digestion and assists the kidneys to filter out waste products.

Meditation

Having got your *yum* and *yeung* balanced, next practise meditation. This is

100

sometimes difficult to explain; the student has to reach the correct physical level before the purpose of meditation can be grasped. Martial art without meditation produces master technicians but not true martial artists. Technicians can copy the elementary physical principles of what they see but understand nothing of its real meaning.

To be successful at meditation, you need will, or *ye*. There are many ways to develop your will. In traditional Chinese schools the good teacher helped the student achieve mental readiness paradoxically by appearing to be unkind or uncaring, neglecting praise in favour of unremitting criticism. This has the effect of concentrating the mind away from the mundane and on to the training itself.

The master might tell a student to fetch water from the village pump. Typically, the martial arts club was situated on the brow of a hill and the water was carried in conical buckets which could not be set down without spilling the contents. Consequently the unfortunate student had to toil the whole way up the hill with no respite whatsoever. Such training is a marvellous way to quieten the mind in preparation for meditation. You can be sure that the struggling, perspiring, aching student was not worrying too much about what he had to do when he got home from training. The front door of the far-off training hall eclipsed all other thoughts.

Using the power of the will, meditation opens the door to a state in which the mind is quiet. Do not confuse this with sleep because the mind is never still then. If you feel relaxed after eight hours of strenuous dreaming, think how good you could feel after only one hour of absolute mental quiet.

Through meditation you quieten the clamour of your thoughts. Some people sit down to meditate but I prefer to stand. I let my body relax totally, breathe with my diaphragm, and let my mind drain of conscious thoughts.

At first, the student consciously tries to suppress his thoughts. This of itself requires thought, so it is self-defeating. The harder you try not to think, the more active your mind becomes. Your imagination is very inventive and soon finds a way around the thought shield you are trying to erect. This conscious thought pressure is generated from the *yeung*. To counter it, visualise a stretch of calm, dark water, and try to feel its coldness. This visualisation is a source of *yum* essence that will help you neutralise thought pressure and attain quiet.

During true meditation, the respiration and pulse both slow. There are adepts who need not breathe for several minutes because their vital energy is at such a high level that it can extract far more oxygen from the air in the lungs than is normal for most people. The air we breathe out is only slightly different from the air we breathe in; the lungs keep only a small part of the available oxygen.

During deep meditation, it is also claimed that breakdown of the body's waste materials proceeds more thoroughly and consequently the adept is less bothered with calls of nature. It is even claimed that meditation can affect the libido to the extent where one is no longer controlled by the desires of the body. Yet when there is a conscious decision to express those desires, they resume with greater potency than before.

Practical exercises

I recommend six sets of traditional exercises to improve your health. They are concerned with whole body health and will have useful spin-offs in terms of endurance and suppleness. Western exercises are not essential to the proper practice of wing chun kuen. Their very nature seems biased in favour of younger, agile people, but not all students of wing chun kuen are beautiful young things. The exercises I recommend are suitable for people of all ages and shapes.

FIG 169

FIG 170

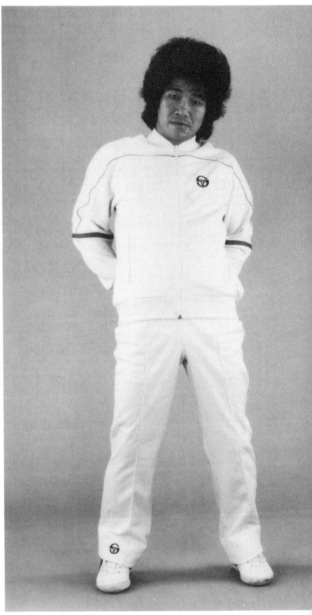

Begin by standing with your feet slightly more than a shoulder-width apart and press with your thumbs on either side of your lower spine (*fig 169*). Maintain this pressure and thrust your hips forward, so your back is well arched (*fig 170*). This stretches the muscles over the stomach. Rotate your hips in a wide circle but do not push your backside out too far (*fig 171, 172*). Feel your trunk muscles pulling at every point as you do 40 rotations one way, then 40 the other. Do not forget to keep pressing with your thumbs.

FIG 171

FIG 172

FIG 173   FIG 174   FIG 175

The next exercise consists of trunk circling. Stand as for the first with your
arms forward *(fig 173)*. Reach with both arms above your shoulders and
hands palm upwards. Reach up and back behind you *(fig 174)*, then
sweep your upper body around in as wide a circle as you can manage *(fig
175, 176, 177, 178)*. Move smoothly and avoid jerking. This exercise is
called *tin* by Chinese teachers.

FIG 176

FIG 177

FIG 178

FIG 179   FIG 180   FIG 181

If you glanced at the third exercise, called *day*, you might think it was a spot of *tai chi chuan* ('great ultimate fist'). Actually it has nothing to do with that system; what resemblance there is, is coincidental.

Take up a stance where the soles of both feet are flat on the floor and weight is biased over the back leg. Put your hands close together with palms downwards and fingers hooked, as though you were pushing a tray *(fig 180)*. Transfer body weight forwards over the front leg *(fig 181)* and push out diagonally with your extended arms as far as you can. Keep both feet flat on the floor and bend your knees. The path your hands describe is a horizontal circle made as wide as possible *(fig 182)*. Draw back, returning weight to your back leg while smoothly withdrawing both arms close to the body *(fig 183)*. Repeat the exercise 16 times, then change the leading leg and and repeat it in a different direction *(fig 184, 185, 186, 187)*.

FIG 182

FIG 183

FIG 184

FIG 185

FIG 186

FIG 187

FIG 188   FIG 189   FIG 190

Start the fourth exercise by standing with the palms of your hands one above the other on the side of your body *(fig 188)*. Bring your weight back so it lies over the rear foot. Move both arms in perfect unison, keeping the palms a constant distance apart. Take them upwards and forwards from the body, as though you were turning a large wheel *(fig 189, 190)*. Reach as far forward as you can, stretching your arms almost straight, then continue the cirlce and draw both arms back to the starting position *(fig 191, 192, 193)*. Take care not to lean forwards with your body and keep both feet firmly on the floor.

During the circle, the arms move diagonally away from the body and not straight out from it. Do this exercise 16 times and then change legs *(fig 194, 195, 196)*. Remember to move smoothly throughout. This exercise is called *yun*.

FIG 191

FIG 192

FIG 193

FIG 194

FIG 195

FIG 196

FIG 197

FIG 198

The fifth exercise, which is specific to wing chun kuen, is an adaptation of moves from one of the advanced training forms. Begin by leaning forward and pushing the hands to the floor *(fig 197)*. Keep the palms pressed together and do not bend the knees. Try to bend from the lower back. Straighten your back and return to upright *(fig 198)*. At the same time press the backs of your hands together and bring them vertically up the front of your chest until just past chest height *(fig 199)*. Then let them split to either side of the head, linking up again above it *(fig 200)*.

Let both hands separate and move down in a big circle with palms held forwards *(fig 201)*. Gather them in at the chest *(fig 202)* and thrust downwards again to repeat the exercise. This exercise must be performed vigorously and quickly.

110

FIG 199

FIG 200

FIG 201

FIG 202

The sixth exercise uses forced exhalation of breath as you thrust both hands palm forwards in front of your chest. Bring them back while breathing in and then thrust them out again, but this time lower down. Move your arms quickly and in unison but do not tense the muscles. Pay close attention to the stance and try to tighten your perineum. This is quite specific in its effect upon the *dan tien* and the flow of *jing*.

Breathing is important. You breathe with your diaphragm; the chest hardly moves at all. When you exhale, you do not blast air out of the lungs but use the diaphragm instead.

If you train regularly with this programme of exercises, the controlled exertion will invigorate the whole body, making you ready for training.

We Chinese have known about specialised training for hundreds of years. If you go to a western specialist in exercise physiology and ask him for an exercise to increase the speed of your punch, he will suggest that you use a speed assisted system. This means facing wallbars and grasping one end of a strong elastic. Tie the other end to the wallbars and position yourself so you can pull back on the elastic until your arm is cocked, ready to punch. Then let your elbow relax and punch. The pull of the elastic speeds the punch and repetition of this exercise leads to a faster delivery.

Traditional wing chun kuen training used bent bamboo canes for training spear hand in almost exactly the same say. You had to choose the correct canes of course, otherwise your assisted spearhand might not stop at the natural length of your arm. I have practised this system and find it very effective, if a little strenuous. I have also used wrist and ankle weights but would caution you against any over-enthusiastic training with aids such as these. Try not to jar the arm repeatedly straight against the natural limit of the elbow or very soon you will permanently damage the joint.

Running is useful for developing overall fitness but start off well inside your limits and gradually build up distance as your fitness level improves. Any form of low intensity but sustained exercise is good because it creates demands in the muscles for more oxygen. To meet demand, blood has to circulate more quickly. This is achieved by elevating the pulse and increasing the force of each contraction. The lungs have to work faster too.

The value of this kind of regime is that it exercises the heart which, like any other muscle, can become flabby if underused.

Exercises like running get the muscles working at a higher level than normal. Active muscles are well supplied with oxygen, and waste materials are quickly eliminated, so they are less susceptible to injury.

Good training!

Some advice on safe practice

'A mistake is not serious unless it is repeated.'

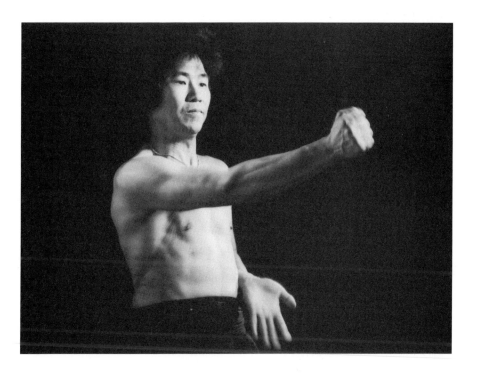

Begin safe practice by joining a safe club, where the instructor is competent to teach properly. The Chinese martial arts contain hundreds of different schools and it is very difficult for the novice to assess which is good and which bad. In a good school, the teacher will be properly trained to coach you, using effective teaching methods that will bring you on quickly. Moreover, the instructor will be accredited with both the British governing body and his own school.

Anyone can go to a sports shop and buy a black belt. With the aid of a black fibretip pen, the most convincing-looking fake certificates can be designed using nothing more esoteric than the menu of the local Chinese take-away. There are students who, after only a short time, consider themselves experts and leave their instructor to found their own schools. Because of their poor skill, they are unable to keep students, and so the process goes on, with the result that there is some pretty dubious Chinese martial art practised. My own style of wing chun kuen has not been exempt from this.

So rule one is to make sure that the instructor of a club is competent. This is not as difficult as it might appear. Fortunately there is a governing body for the Chinese martial arts in Britain, the British Kung Fu Council. Would-be students of the Chinese martial arts are strongly urged to check the bona fides of a potential club by contacting the British Kung Fu

Council at 1st Floor, Broadway House, 15–16 Deptford Broadway, London SE8 4PE. Be sure to enclose a stamped, addressed envelope. The Council is a founder member of the Martial Arts Commission which controls all the martial arts in Britain.

Membership of the British Kung Fu Council provides you with international recognition and a valuable insurance policy which protects not only you but also the people with whom you train. Wing chun kuen is a martial art and even in the best run schools accidents cannot be totally ruled out. Your governing body insurance policy will provide you with a weekly benefit payment if you suffer injury and a capital sum if that injury is likely to last a long time.

Perhaps more important is third party indemnity in case you inadvertently injure someone during training. Unfortunately court actions are on the increase and this kind of policy is a wise precaution. All British Kung Fu Council instructors have a professional indemnity policy which covers them against claims arising out of their negligence while teaching. Should you have any complaint against a registered instructor, the British Kung Fu Council will look into it and report back to you.

Approved clubs will meet certain safety criteria observed by the Council. They include such things as specifications for the floor in the training hall. Wing chun kuen is a vigorous martial art and, from time to time, people fall over during training. For this reason, the floor must be resilient; solid

floors are out because they are known to cause or contribute to injury. Approved clubs will not have any unpadded pillars or radiators for you to bang up against. Light fittings will be out of harm's way and windows will be well back from the training area or properly screened with wire mesh. The approved instructor will take care to ensure that the training area is never overcrowded.

When you start training in a recognised club which follows these guidelines, you will develop aches in places you never knew you had. This is because the techniques used in wing chun kuen exercise muscles to a degree and in a manner they are not used to. The extent to which this incapacitates you depends on how fit you are to start with. To avoid overdoing things, do not pace your training against other people but set your own limits and work within them. The class will contain some students who are fitter than you and some who are not as fit, so concentrate on improving your own pace.

If you are in any doubt about your health, see your doctor and have a medical check-up. This especially important if you are over 40. Sudden unaccustomed training can reveal hitherto unsuspected health deficiencies. Do not train on a full stomach because the blood circulation demands on digestion have a priority above that of the muscles, including the muscle of the heart. Allow two hours after eating a light meal before you begin training.

Make sure you tell your instructor about any health problems you have. This will allow him to monitor your training and be prepared for any difficulties which may arise. It is perfectly all right for you to train if you suffer from asthma – in fact, regular wing chun kuen practice can improve the condition. Through a preoccupation with training, you will tend to overlook early symptoms of breathlessness that make you apprehensive. You will come to realise that breathlessness is not necessarily a sign of an impending attack but can be the normal shortness of breath experienced by any hard-training martial artist. Nevertheless, make sure you have your medication with you and do not be afraid to drop out of training to take it.

People with heart conditions can also gain great benefit from training. The cardiac sufferer can train, subject to advice from his doctor, but he should be careful to stay well within his limits. Some conditions give warning twinges when the heart is under stress and the student must be encouraged to ease up when they occur. It is not clever to try to exercise through the pain barrier.

Epileptics can train provided the instructor knows about the condition. The usual type of epileptic attack involves nothing more than a momentary loss of awareness or concentration, and if the sufferer is left to himself he soon comes out of it and resumes training. Full seizures are very rare, but someone who is prone to them should make sure that the club where he trains has a soft floor, in case he falls and bangs his head.

Diabetics know their insulin requirements, but wing chun kuen training can sometimes catch them unawares and their blood sugar level may drop. The forewarned instructor will notice the diabetic student becoming confused or irrational. I once knew a student who, for no apparent reason, would suddenly become very aggressive, whereas normally he was a quiet individual. I found out later that he was a diabetic and his aggressive interludes always occurred when his blood sugar dropped during sustained training.

Haemophilia is the one condition that cannot be tolerated in wing chun kuen training. The unfortunate sufferers from this hereditary disease are

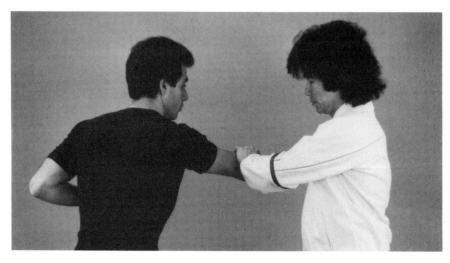

deficient in blood clotting factors and any injury results in a large loss of blood. In some cases, hospital attention is needed to stop bleeding. The mere action of punching or kicking, without actually hitting anything, can cause damage to joint capsules. This is well tolerated in the healthy person but the haemophiliac can bleed internally into the joint, causing a painful and damaging immobility.

Be careful of injuries sustained during training and make sure you let the instructor know about them, especially if you have suffered a hard blow to the head. Sometimes the injury is severe enough to cause momentary loss of contact with the senses. The sufferer may not fall down or even totter, but he may be unable to respond properly to a question. In such cases he must be withdrawn from violent activity and not allowed to fight or run the risk of further head injury for six weeks after the accident.

This rather severe action is taken because injuries to the brain are cumulative. Medical research has shown that accumulated head injuries can have distressing symptoms lasting for months.

Do not come to training if you have a virus infection. Certain types of viruses irritate the heart muscle and cause it to behave abnormally when suddenly stimulated. It is theoretically possible for a punch which jars the chest to cause an interruption in heart rhythm.

Always begin the training session with a series of warm-up exercises. During everyday activity the body operates at a level sufficient to meet routine demands. However, wing chun kuen training involves greater demands and a carefully followed warm-up programme will gradually raise the body's metabolic level to cope with them. If this is done gradually, there will be less physical distress, and an increased flow of blood to the muscles will lead to more effective training.

During the operation of muscles, a waste product called lactic acid is formed. The muscle can tolerate quite a high concentration before its action is impaired and stiffening sets in. If you go beyond this limit, the muscle eventually becomes exhausted and loses the power to contract. At the end of a session any well-exercised muscle will contain lactic acid which should be dispersed as far as possible by a sensible series of cool-down exercises.

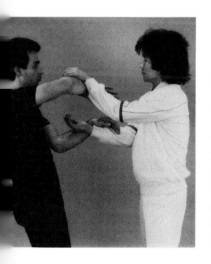

If the exercises are light enough, the muscle's natural pumping action expels a lot of the lactic acid. The cool-down also allows the muscle to pump out the large volumes of fluid which accumulate naturally in it during the active phase. If fluid is not dispersed, swelling can occur.

In both warm-up and cool-down, use exercises such as running on the spot and standing jumps. Finish each session with stretching exercises, taking a joint through its full range of movement. The limiting factors to joint movement are largely the tension and length of the muscle involved. If the muscle can be relaxed and lengthened, the range of movement is automatically increased.

The state of stretch of any joint is perceived through messages sent from the spindle organs found in the tendons and muscles. It is possible to fool these by taking the joint to its limit, then tightening the muscles involved.

Hold the contraction for a count of ten, then release. The joint will now move a little more. Whatever you do, never force your joints by swinging heavy weights on them or using someone else to apply extra leverage. This can result in torn muscles and damaged tendons which can take a long time to repair.

It is very important to keep your cool when training with a partner. With the best will in the world, slip-ups can happen; you must be prepared to take them in your stride. If things start to get a little out of hand, stop training immediately and back off. When you are asked to find a partner, pick someone of your own size – technical standard is not so important. If you train with a more skilled person, you will benefit from his instruction. If your partner is less skilled than you, you will gain a good insight into techniques through correcting his mistakes.

During sparring take extra care if your partner is significantly larger or smaller than you are. Larger people generate a great deal of force simply through their mass. Without apparent effort, they can strike quite hard. The smaller person with lighter bones may find training with them rather hazardous.

Remember always to do the technique shown by the teacher and do not be tempted to vary it. Some wing chun kuen techniques are potentially dangerous, so take this into account.

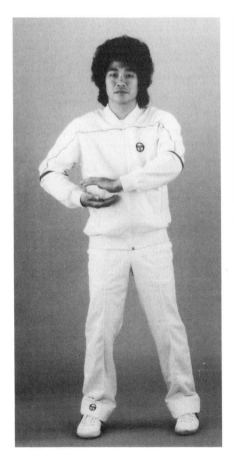

Philosophy and practice of wing chun kuen

'Man has learned to fly like the birds. Now all he has to work out is how to do it as quietly.'

Wing chun kuen training begins and ends with courtesy. The people who come to training sessions want to be there; all members of the class are one family, wanting one thing – to learn wing chun kuen. To learn well, they must depend not only on the teacher but also on each other. Each session should start with the students assembling into an orderly class and greeting each other and the teacher with the formal salutation. Momentarily hold the knuckles of your right fist against the palm of your left hand, at the level of the upper chest, to signal 'hello', 'thank you', and 'good-bye'.

Use the salutation when entering and leaving class, even temporarily. Do not come in or go out without asking the teacher and never interrupt him by word or action while he is talking to the class. If you are late, do not walk in unbidden. Make sure the teacher can see you, then stand politely until you are admitted.

Use the salutation if you see a colleague outside the training hall. It identifies you as a member of a school in which you take pride. Use the same salutation for all classes of people. Whether you are a bank manager or unemployed, you and your classmates depend on each other and you therefore give respect. If you do not respect your classmates, how can you respect yourself? You are all practising the same art.

An inexpensive training uniform is another way of sweeping away social and sexual distinctions. You can train in your everday clothes if you want, but they will end up sweaty, uncomfortable, and perhaps damaged. It is better to have clothes set aside specifically for training. Typically these will be a T-shirt or sweatshirt (depending on the temperature), a pair of loose dark trousers, lightweight white socks, and kung fu slippers. Do not practise barefoot becaue you can pick up splinters and perhaps even a foot condition such as verrucae.

Never stand around with hands in pockets, lounge against the wall, or sprawl over the floor. Make a conscious effort to discipline yourself because the techniques you learn are dangerous, especially if misused, and can cause serious injury. There is a particularly apt saying that 'If you cannot obey, you cannot command'. This is certainly true of wing chun kuen training.

If the teacher is explaining some point, the students should gather round him attentively. Do not sit down unless told to do so. The teacher may ask certain students to come forward and demonstrate a particular part of their training to the class. The purpose of this is to allow classmates to assess the standard and see how the teacher corrects mistakes. This gives them an insight into their own training.

Too much analysis can stand in the way of training. If you analyse techniques too closely, you will miss their true meaning. Consider the flower; it is beautiful to look at and to smell, so why become preoccupied with classifying it? This preoccupation with needless detail leads to a mind so obsessed with trivia that it cannot see the wood for the trees. Once you classify the flower, once you reduce it to a concept – that's it. There is an eventual limit to available knowledge but none at all to the imagination which springs from the spirit, the *ye*.

If your *ye* is strong, you can achieve miracles. The phenomenon of hysterical strength is well known. Many of us have heard how a mother has lifted a car wheel to get at her child trapped beneath. Medical science, which is obsessed with classification, will tell you that this achieved through hypermobilisation of the musculature, but that is only giving names to the flower. The woman never thought, 'Can I lift that car wheel to rescue my child?' She just did it.

Accepting challenges plays a vital role in cultivating *ye*. By means of long and austere training, the body and mind are challenged to meet and exceed their limits. When you exceed your natural capabilities injury sometimes results, but this is not always to your detriment. There are many forms of injury which one must suffer. For example, when a child walks barefoot on a rough surface, his skin is damaged and it responds to this injury by thickening over the injured areas.

Sometimes injuries serve another purpose. They act as signposts for your future development and, if you are a teacher, for the guidance of students. You will not make the same mistake twice and your understanding and knowledge consequently improve. As a corollary, beware of the teacher who has accepted no challenges and made no mistakes. With no knowledge of the pitfalls, how can he advise others to avoid them?

The martial arts are not a finished product; they are still evolving as students reach the limits of present training and then break through them. It is precisely because of this evolution that study of the martial arts takes a lifetime. There is always something to be learned and limits to be pushed back. Today's goals exist only so we can exceed them tomorrow.

Most people take up martial arts as a leisure activity. For such students the be-all and end-all of training is the coveted coloured belt awarded after each grading examination. They take pleasure in trivial things, mistakenly measuring their progress against another's yardstick. To them, the true depths of the martial arts may never reveal themselves.

The martial arts are an art form whose study enriches the imagination and improves the quality of life. The ultimate aim of the martial artist is to use his training to become a master of life and so lay hold of the art of living. Masters in any art must first be masters of living, for the soul creates everything.

Terminology used in kung fu

'Knowing others is wisdom; knowing self is
enlightenment. Mastering others requires
force; mastering self requires strength.'

Acupuncture A traditional Chinese science which seeks to regulate the flow of *chi* through the body by the placement of needles at various locations.

Advanced A stage of sophistication in training and understanding, reached after a long period of training.

Art A discipline or skill that benefits the mind and body.

Attention stance A formal posture adopted by the student when listening to the teacher.

Augment To strengthen.

Back fist Striking with the upper surface of the knuckles.

Bah jam do Butterfly knives; short slashing knives with a hand guard and single cutting edge.

Bah mei 'White eyebrows'; a style of *kung fu* named after its founder, who had bushy white eyebrows.

Basics Fundamental techniques practised in a simple form.

Bear One of the animals on which styles of *kung fu* are based.

Bear hand A form of claw hand in which bent fingers are used to rake the opponent's face.

Belt A sash, often coloured, denoting the stage practice attained; worn in traditional schools to contain the *chi*.

Bird Two birds are customarily associated with *kung fu*, the crane and the eagle. The study of both has given rise to major *kung fu* styles.

Biu ji Finger jab used in wing chun kuen. It is also the name of the third form.

Biu ma Method of stepping quickly from stance to stance in wing chun kuen.

Black belt A black sash denoting that the wearer has attained a certain degree of competence; not found in traditional schools.

Blocking A technique which diverts an attack from its target by interposing a limb or part of the body in its path.

Bong sau Block with elbow lifted.

Bow stance	A long stance common to northern *wu shu* schools. The front leg is extended and straight; the rear leg is well bent.
Boxing	A form of unarmed combat using kicks and punches as weapons.
Breathing	A key principle from which power is developed. The diaphragm is used, rather than the chest.
Broadsword	A curved, single-edge, long sword used in *wu shu*.
Buddhism	A religious creed which advocates enlightenment through meditation. Chan Yuen Gong Buddhism is commonly associated with the martial arts. Its legendary founder was Tong Sam Jong whose exploits are recorded in *The Water Margin*.
Butterfly kick	A circling kick used in *wu shu*. The sole of the foot is slapped into the palm of the hand.
Butterfly knife	See *bah jam do*.
Centre of gravity	The body's centre of balance, just inward from the navel.
Centre line	An imaginary vertical line which passes from the groin vertically up the trunk, neck, and head.
Chain	An unorthodox weapon consisting of a weighted head attached to a light-link chain.
Chan	The form of Buddhism most commonly associated with martial arts.
Chang chuan	A northern *wu shu* style employing a long-fist form used much in competitions.
Cheung	The spear.
Cheung kiu sau	'Long bridge hand'; a long-range hand technique common to many schools of *kung fu*.
Ching loh	The 12 meridians along which *chi* flows. There are six *yum* meridians and six *yeung*, each corresponding with an hour of the Chinese day. The *yeung* meridians related to active organs of the body, the *yum* meridians to the storage organs.
Chin gum sau	'Front pinning hand'; a wing chun kuen blocking technique.
Chinna	The art of seizing; a grappling system of unarmed combat using armlocks and holds.
Chi sau	'Sticking hands', a wing chun kuen exercise used to develop awareness.
Choke	A technique which restricts a person's breathing or the flow of blood to his brain.
Chop	Vulgar name for a striking technique using the little-finger edge of the hand.
Chow gar	A family style of southern *kung fu* developed from *choy gar* and *hung kuen*.
Choy	One of the five original styles of Shaolin *kung fu*.
Choy gar	Choy family style of *kung fu*.
Choy lee fut	Southern style of *kung fu* using long-hand techniques and swinging punches.
Chuan	A mandarin term meaning 'fist'.
Chuan fa	'Way of the fist'; a term used to describe Chinese boxing.
Chuan shu	'Art of the fist'; a term used to describe *kung fu*.
Chum kiu	'Seeking the bridge'; the second wing chun kuen form which derives its name from its seeking-out of the opponent's weaknesses.
Chum kiu ma	Method of stepping used in wing chun kuen.
Claw	A technique which uses the hooked fingers to rake and/or grasp. A variation uses the thumb and index finger to grasp the windpipe.
Control	Regulation applied to a technique, limiting its force, speed, or delivery.
Co-ordination	Performing several actions concurrently or in sequence to achieve a desired result.
Crane	One of the five animals on which styles of *kung fu* were based. The crane styles rely heavily on distance and evasion.
Crane's beak	A hand technique in which the thumb and tips of fingers are pressed together to form a beak.
Crane stance	A one-legged stance in which the forward foot is raised from the ground.
Crescent kick	A turning kick is delivered with the toes of the kicking foot pointing vertically upwards.
Dai dar	Low blow.
Dai jeung	Low palm strike.
Da jong	Arm-conditioning exercise in which the forearms are swung against wooden spars or other hard objects.

Dan chi	Single-arm sticking hands practice. This is the elementary level of sticking hands practice.
Dan tien	The Cantonese term for *tan tien*.
Da sum sing	An arm-conditioning exercise practised in pairs and involving the reciprocal strong blocks applied to opposing forearms in a repeating sequence. The exercise is derived from the hung kuen school.
Death touch	A secret technique said to cause death even when applied lightly.
Deflect	To redirect an attacking technique, rendering it harmless.
Dim mok	Use of the so-called vital points of the body. See also *death touch*.
Discipline	Self-imposed control intrinsic to a true study of the martial arts.
Distraction	A feint to divert the opponent's attention.
Double palm	Technique sequence found in *pa kua*.
Downward block	Technique applied to low attacks.
Dragon fist	Punch in which the middle knuckle of the third finger is extruded forward.
Drunken style	A sequence of techniques practised in some styles during which the practitioner appears to be drunk or unsteady in order to confuse the attacker.
Duen kiu	'Short bridge hand'; a common short-range technique found in many *kung fu* styles.
Eagle claw	A style of *kung fu* characterised by jumping techniques and claw hand attacks to the eyes.
Edge of foot	The edge of the foot on the little-toe side, used during the side kick.
Edge of hand	The little-finger edge of the hand. Sometimes known as the 'chop'.
Elbow	A useful short-range weapon used as a horizontal or downward vertical strike.
External system	Form of *kung fu* in which the power is mainly generated through the application of purely physical principles. Known also as *wai chia* or *ngoy gar*.
Fist	A weapon formed by closing the fingers against the palm.
Five animals	The dragon, snake, tiger, leopard, and crane are the animals upon which several major styles of *kung fu* are based.
Focus	The point at which the maximum energy of a technique is delivered.
Follow-up	The technique which comes quickly behind another as part of a sequence.
Fook sau	A resilient bent-elbow block used in sticking hands practice.
Forearm	The part of the lower arm between elbow and wrist. It is frequently used in blocks.
Form	A pattern of pre-arranged techniques performed in sequence. See also *pattern*.
Free sparring	A form of sparring where both partners can try out techniques in a simulated fight.
Front kick	A kick which travels forward in a straight line; can be either a snap kick or a thrusting kick.
Front leg kick	A kick delivered from the forward leg.
Fu jow pai	A Shaolin system based on the actions of the tiger. Claw hand is used a great deal.
Garn sau	In wing chun kuen, a lower block; also a double block comprising *jum sau* and *garn sau*.
Gim	Sword.
Go dar	High blow.
Gong	Hard
Gong fu	A Cantonese expression meaning 'good technique'. It is the common name for Chinese martial art, and is the same as *kung fu*.
Grading	A periodic assessment of practice standard measured against a set syllabus. Students wear coloured sashes denoting their grade.
Grappling techniques	Techniques which rely on applying a leverage hold, lock, or throw.
Guard	The interrelationship of hands and feet which provides both an effective defensive screen and a platform for launching attacks.
Gwan	Staff or pole.
Gwan do	A long-handled weapon with an axe-like chopping head.
Hammer fist	A closed-fist technique which impacts with the pad of muscle running between the little finger and the wrist.
Hand conditioning	A form of training which makes the hand's striking surfaces hard enough to deliver a strong technique without causing injury to the user.
Hard style	A synonym for 'external system'.

Heel kick	A technique using the heel of the foot as impact area.
Hok joy	'Crane's beak'; a hand technique used in crane style.
Hooking block	A block in which the hand curls around the attacking technique and grasps it.
Hook punch	A short-distance punch which travels in an arc.
Hop gar	A system of *kung fu* noted for its footwork.
Hsing ye	An internal system of *kung fu*. The term means 'mind boxing'.
Huen sau	Circling wrist block.
Hung gar	An external style of southern *kung fu*.
Hung sing	A variant of *choy lee fut* style of *kung fu*.
I-chin ching	An exercise system said to have been devised by Ta Mo.
I-ching	*The Book of Changes*, an old Chinese form of divination.
I huan	A synonym for *hsing ye*.
Inner power	Also known as *chi*. This force can be generated and focused thereby producing very powerful techniques.
Internal system	'Soft' system of *kung fu*. Also known as *loy gar* and *nei chia*. Does not appear to rely on the application of simple physical strength.
Inward block	A technique in which the attack is deflected with an inward movement of the blocking arm.
Jeen ma	'Arrow walking'; a sequence of advancing or retreating steps practised in wing chun kuen.
Jeet kune do	A system of *kung fu* synthesised by the late Bruce Lee. The term means 'way of the intercepting fist'.
Jing	The natural energy of the healthy body.
Joan dar	Middle blow.
Jong fat	Techniques used against the wooden dummy.
Juk tek	Side kick.
Jum sau	'Sinking block'; a powerful wing chun kuen technique which uses the little-finger side of the forearm.
Jut sau	Deflecting hand.
Kan shu	Method of hand conditioning in which the hand is thrust hard into various mixtures of increasing abrasion.
Kao sau	A short version of the wing chun kuen block, *gan sau*.
Kicking	Impact technique delivered by the foot.
Kiu sau ma bo	The interrelationship of guard and stance that enables the expert to assess the capabilities of a boxer on appearance alone.
Knee	Short-range leg technique used against the opponent's groin or thigh.
Knife hand	A synonym for 'Chop'. The fingers must be held rigid during delivery.
Kuen	Cantonese for 'fist'.
Kung fu	See *gong fu*.
Kuo shu	The martial arts of China.
Kwai jan	A downwards-travelling elbow strike.
Kwan sau	A double block, made up of *tan sau* and lower *bong sau*.
Kwoon	Training hall or club.
Lan sau	'Bar arm'; a wing chun kuen technique used to fend off.
Lap gwa choy	Back fist.
Lap sau	Grabbing hand.
Lau gar	A Siu Lum system developed by the Lau family.
Law horn kuen	Style of *kung fu* characterised by jumping techniques and intricate footwork.
Light contact	An expression which refers to controlled techniques stopping well short of a forceful delivery.
Ling wood	Very supple and fast.
Long hand boxing	A collective term used to describe those styles of *kung fu* which use long-range hand techniques.
Loy gar	Cantonese name for the internal styles of *kung fu*.
Loy mun kuen	Inside gate punch.
Loy pak	Inside slapping block.
Loy sing	Perseverence.
Luk dim boon kwan	'Six and a half pole techniques'; a wing chun kuen training system used to develop power.
Ma bo	Stance or posture.
Man sau	'Inquisitive arm'; a wing chun kuen technique during which the guard is raised to meet an attack. It is named after Yip Man.
Martial	Military, pertaining to war.
Martial art	The application of military techniques.

Master	A person who has achieved a high standard of technical competence.
Mo hay	Traditional *kung fu* weapons.
Mo soot	Martial art; – *wu shu* in Mandarin.
Mok gar	A style of southern *kung fu*.
Monkey style	A style of *kung fu* in which the movements of the monkey are reproduced by the practitioner. There are various forms of monkey style.
Mook yan jong	Wooden dummy used during training, with spars projecting at differing angles to represent the arms and an angled lower spar representing the knee.
Mui fa jeong	A series of tree stumps, driven into the ground at varying heights, on which footwork is practised.
Multiple attack	A sequence of techniques.
Nei chia	The internal styles of *kung fu*; the principal ones are *tai chi chuan, pa kua*, and *hsing ye*.
Ngoy gar	Cantonese term for external systems of *kung fu*.
Northern styles	The *kung fu* schools of northern China. Typically these use high kicks and jumping techniques.
Pa kua	The 'eight trigrams' style of internal *kung fu*. The practitioner rapidly circles the opponent, changing direction with great speed.
Pak dar	Simultaneous block and attack.
Pak hok	The *kung fu* style based on the crane. The term 'pak hok' means 'crane'.
Pak sau	'Slapping block'; a wing chun kuen blocking technique.
Palm heel	The base of the palm.
Pattern	A series of prearranged techniques performed in sequence. See also *form*.
Peng chuan	The 'crushing fist' of *hsing ye kung fu*.
Pi chuan	The 'splitting fist' of *hsing ye kung fu*.
Pie jan	Horizontal elbow strike.
Po pi cheung	A double palm attack used in wing chun kuen.
Posture	The attitude of the body during practice.
Praying mantis	A widespread style of external *kung fu*; also known as *tong long*.
Pressure points	Places on the body which, when pressed or struck, produce a response out of all proportion to the force used.
Punch	Hand technique delivered with the fingers wholly or partially rolled into the palm.

Range	The distance between opponents.
Rank	The level of proficiency of a practitioner.
Recoil	The reverse-travelling reaction produced when a technique impacts on a target.
Rising block	A deflection technique that redirects a strike to the face or head by means of a diagonal lifting movement of the blocking arm.
Salutation	A greeting exchanged between practitioners. Between a class and teacher, the front of the fist is pushed into the palm. Between one stylist and another, the little-finger side of the fist is pressed into the palm of the hand. Between masters of different styles, the fist is clasped by the palm.
Sam kok ma	'Triangular steps'; a method of stepping in wing chun kuen.
Sash	A belt, sometimes coloured to denote the rank of the wearer.
Sau fat	Hand techniques.
School	A particular method or style of practising *kung fu*.
Seven stars	A variety of praying mantis style of *kung fu*.
Shaolin	The Buddhist temple in Hunan province where the legendary Ta Mo introduced the principles of Chan Yuen Jong Buddhism to the practice of martial art.
Sheung chi	Double sticking hand practice.
Si bak	The instructor's senior colleague.
Si dai	The student who joined the class later and is consequently junior.
Si fu	The instructor.
Si gung	The instructor's teacher.
Si hing	The student who joined the class earlier and is consequently senior.
Si jo	The founder of a style of *kung fu*.
Si sook	The instructor's junior colleague.
Side kick	A stamping kick delivered with the side of the foot and heel.
Siu lim tao	'Little idea'; the first wing chun kuen form, practice of which will give you an insight to the style.
Siu Lum	The Cantonese name for Shaolin.
Soft style	A synonym for internal systems.
Southern styles	Schools of *kung fu* developed in southern China and characterised by solid stances and hand techniques.
Sparring	An exchange of unprogrammed techniques; see also *Free sparring*.

Spear hand	Open-handed technique using the tips of the fingers. See also *biu ji*.
Staff	A hardwood pole used to develop power in *kung fu* techniques.
Stance	Body posture used in practice.
Sticking hands	Close-range practice with a partner in wing chun kuen. The partners press their forearms together and try to sense each other's impending attack. Also called *chi sau*.
Style	An interpretation of *kung fu* practice. See also *school*.
Tactics	Use of techniques and attitudes to achieve an advantage.
Tai chi chuan	'Great ultimate fist'; an internal form of *kung fu* characterised by its gentle, relaxed movements.
Tai gik kuen	The Cantonese rendering of *tai chi chuan*.
Ta Mo	The Indian monk who introduced Chan Buddhism to the Shaolin temple. He is credited with combining martial art with religious discipline to produce shaolin temple boxing.
Tan dar	Simultaneous palm-up block and punch.
Tan sau	Palm-up block.
Tan tien	The centre of *chi* production in the viscera. Also known as *dan tien*. There are three separate locations – one in the forehead, one in the chest, and one in the stomach.
Tao	The term used to describe the endlessly repeating cycles of macro- and microcosm.
Toh dai	Students.
Toh suen	The students of a student.
Tong long	Praying mantis style of *kung fu*.
Uniform	A formal tunic worn by a style of *kung fu*.
Upward block	The same as 'rising block.'
Vital points	The areas of the body which, when stimulated, can cause death or injury.
Wai chia	The external systems of *kung fu*.
Wang jeung	Sideways palm strike.
Wing chun kuen	'Beautiful springtime', a style of *kung fu* said to have been developed by the Buddhist nun Ng Mui and taught to Yim Wing Chun.
Wu dang	An ancient style of *kung fu*.
Wu sau	Protective guard.
Wu shu	The Mandarin term for martial art.
Yang	The Mandarin term for *yeung*.
Yan jeung	Thrusting palm strike.
Yao	Soft.
Yee jee kim yeung ma	Straddle stance.
Yeung	The principle of light, fire, and air. Commonly associated with the male.
Yin	The Mandarin term for *yum*.
Yum	The principle of darknesss, water, and coolness. Commonly associated with the female.

Acknowledgements

Several people helped me to write this book and I would here like to record my thanks to them.

First I thank my wife, Marianne, for her patience with my bad English and her skill in making the text readable, through inspired editing.

Secondly I want to thank my friend David Mitchell who, like me, is a martial artist and knew which questions would draw the best response from the knowledge I possess. He also helped me produce the text.

My student Danny Loizos kindly assisted me in the photographs and I thank him for his efforts to promote wing chun kuen in this respect.

Finally I would like to thank all the people who helped me during my visit and research at the Futshan Temple, mainland China.

SL